Grammar Basics Plus
Level B

Published by LDA
an imprint of

Author: Margaret Fetty
Editor: Rebecca Warren

Published by LDA
An imprint of McGraw-Hill Children's Publishing

Send all inquiries to:
McGraw-Hill Children's Publishing
3195 Wilson Drive NW
Grand Rapids, Michigan 49544

Grammar Basics Plus, Level B
ISBN: 0-7424-1857-X

1 2 3 4 5 6 7 8 9 PHXBK 09 08 07 06 05 04 03

The McGraw-Hill Companies

Table of Contents

How to Use This Book

As students struggle to develop reading and writing fluency, it helps to bring them "back to basics." *Grammar Basics Plus* provides a thorough introduction to the building blocks of language. The book is divided into three units—Parts of Speech, Usage, and Mechanics. Each unit contains two-page lesson spreads on essential skills. These stand-alone pages can be used individually or together.

To help facilitate student understanding, lessons include alternating nonfiction and fiction selections. Giving students practice using grammar in a variety of genres encourages deeper understanding. Both pages in a lesson (nonfiction and fiction) are on a similar topic, making it easy for students to work through the problems. Rather than having to change gears for each question, students move easily through sentences that naturally flow together. Working within one topic also helps focus student attention.

Use the checklist of skills on page 5 to monitor student progress. You may want to check off each lesson as students complete it or wait to check it off until you are confident the skill has been mastered. Each unit ends with assessment pages. Use these before students begin working as a tool for discovering weak areas or after students have done the lessons to track skill development.

Modify these pages as individual student needs require. Some suggested modifications are listed below.

- On pages where students are to fill in blanks from a word box, cut out the words and have the student paste them on the correct line.
- Rather than circling the correct answer, have your students use a highlighter to mark the answers.
- Use a variety of colored highlighters to identify similar components on each page—one color for a definition, one for an example, and so on.
- Use a photocopier to enlarge the pages. Then cut or rearrange the elements to make them even clearer.
- Create a word wall, listing words under their correct part of speech. Add to this as students work through the skills in this book.

With the help of this book, even struggling learners will gain confidence with grammar, acquiring a solid foundation for reading and writing success.

Name ______________________________ Date ______________________

Checklist of Skills

Unit 1: Parts of Speech

Nouns

- ❑ What Is a Noun?
- ❑ Common Nouns
- ❑ Proper Nouns
- ❑ Singular and Plural Nouns
- ❑ Plural Nouns
- ❑ Possessive Nouns

Verbs

- ❑ What Is a Verb?
- ❑ Verbs
- ❑ Linking Verbs
- ❑ Helping Verbs
- ❑ The Verb *Be (Am, Is,* and *Are)*
- ❑ The Verb *Be (Was* and *Were)*
- ❑ Present Tense Verbs
- ❑ Past Tense Verbs
- ❑ Future Tense Verbs
- ❑ Verb Agreement
- ❑ Irregular Verbs

Pronouns

- ❑ What Is a Pronoun?
- ❑ Subject and Object Pronouns
- ❑ Possessive Pronouns
- ❑ Demonstrative Pronouns
- ❑ Interrogative Pronouns
- ❑ Antecedents

Adjectives

- ❑ What Is an Adjective?
- ❑ Adjectives That Compare

Adverbs

- ❑ Adverbs
- ❑ Use *Good* and *Well*

Prepositions

- ❑ Prepositions

Conjunctions

- ❑ Conjunctions
- ❑ Simple and Complex Sentences

Interjections

- ❑ Interjections

Unit 2: Usage

- ❑ Subject and Verb Agreement
- ❑ Verb Tense
- ❑ Irregular Verbs
- ❑ Pronouns and Antecedents
- ❑ Prefixes
- ❑ Suffixes
- ❑ Synonyms
- ❑ Antonyms
- ❑ Compound Words
- ❑ Homophones
- ❑ Homographs
- ❑ Troublesome Words
- ❑ Contractions
- ❑ Double Negatives

Unit 3: Mechanics

- ❑ Sentence Endings
- ❑ Commas
- ❑ Quotations Marks
- ❑ Proper Names
- ❑ Abbreviations of Names and Places
- ❑ Abbreviations of Days and Months
- ❑ Names of Holidays and Historical Events
- ❑ Titles
- ❑ Difficult Words

Name ______________________ Date ______________

What Is a Noun?

Many words name things. Naming words are called **nouns**. Nouns can name a person, place, or thing.

Examples:

Person: A rancher has many responsibilities.
Place: The ranch is a busy place.
Thing: A rancher raises cattle.

Directions: Read the sentences. Look at the underlined word in each sentence. Write if the noun names a **person**, a **place**, or a **thing**.

1. A ranch may also raise sheep. ______________

2. There are too many animals to live in a barnyard. ______________

3. The animals live on large areas of land. ______________

4. Sometimes, cowboys round up the cattle. ______________

5. The cowboys move the animals to another field. ______________

6. The animals will have tall grass to eat. ______________

0-7424-1857-X *Grammar Basics Plus*

Name ______________________________ Date ______________

What Is a Noun?

A **noun** is a word that names a person, a place, or a thing.

Directions: Read the story. Look at the underlined words. Write each word in the column to tell if it is a **person**, a **place**, or a **thing**.

Pecos Bill Invents the Lasso

Pecos Bill was living in the woods. One day, he met a man who told him about Texas. Texas was a land filled with lots of cattle and cowboys. Pecos decided to head to the great state of Texas.

As Bill crossed the desert, a rattlesnake wrapped itself around his body. Bill got a hand free and squeezed the snake. Before long, the snake became thin and limp like a rope. Bill rolled up the snake and continued on his way.

When Bill got to Texas, he saw lots of longhorn cattle. Bill had never seen a cow with such long, sharp horns, so he walked up to get a closer look. Longhorns didn't like people to get too close. The cow began to charge straight toward Bill. Bill quickly pulled out his snake and swung it in a circle around his head. Bill let the snake fly, caught the head of the longhorn, and wrestled the longhorn to the ground. The lasso had been invented.

Person	Place	Thing
______	______	______
______	______	______
______	______	______

Name ______________________________ Date ____________________

Common Nouns

A **noun** is a word that names a person, a place, or a thing.

Examples:

Person: What do people do when they are hungry?
Place: Some people go to a restaurant.
Thing: They can order food at a restaurant.

Directions: Read the sentences. Underline the noun in each sentence. Write if the noun names a **person**, a **place**, or a **thing**.

1. You can find restaurants along streets. ____________________

2. Some restaurants are inside shopping malls. ____________________

3. A menu lists all kinds of food. ____________________

4. A waiter writes the food order. ____________________

5. The waiter takes the order to the kitchen. ____________________

6. The waiter comes back with a plate full of delicious food.

____

0-7424-1857-X *Grammar Basics Plus*

Name ______________________________ Date ____________________

Common Nouns

A **noun** is a word that names a person, a place, or a thing.

Directions: Read the story. Write nouns from the box to complete the sentences.

paper	judge	pie	bakery
fair	friends	winner	prize

The Pie Contest

Mei stood beside her apple **(1)** ______________. She watched the **(2)** ______________ get a spoon and take a small bite. He scribbled some notes on his pad of **(3)** ______________ and moved on.

This was the first time Mei had entered a pie in the county **(4)** ______________ food contest. All of her **(5)** ______________ said she made the best apple pies. Mei didn't care about winning first **(6)** ______________. She just wanted a ribbon.

Finally, the judge had sampled all of the pies. "All the pies were very good," the judge said. "But there was one that had a flaky crust and rich apple taste. The **(7)** ______________ of the contest this year is Mei Parker! In fact, I hope I can convince Mei to come work in my **(8)** ______________ each Saturday."

Mei smiled and clapped. Not only did she win first prize; she got a job, too.

0-7424-1857-X *Grammar Basics Plus*

Name ______________________________ Date ______________

Proper Nouns

A **noun** is a word that names a person, a place, or a thing. A **proper noun** names a special person, place, or thing. All proper nouns begin with capital letters. Some proper nouns are made with more than one word.

Example: Amelia Earhart was an airplane pilot.

proper noun (Amelia Earhart) — common noun (pilot)

Directions: Read the sentences. Underline the proper noun in each sentence. (Hint: There may be two proper nouns in some sentences.)

1. Amelia was born in Kansas in 1897.
2. She moved to California in 1920.
3. She took flying lessons from a woman named Neta Snook.
4. Amelia was the first woman to fly alone across the Atlantic Ocean.
5. She flew in a Vega airplane.
6. Amelia wanted to fly around the world.
7. She started her trip in the United States.
8. Amelia was last seen flying over the country of New Guinea.

Name ______________________________ Date ______________

Proper Nouns

A **proper noun** names a special person, place, or thing. All proper nouns begin with capital letters. Some proper nouns are made with more than one word.

Directions: Read the letter. Write your own proper nouns to complete the sentences. The first one is done for you.

Dear **(1)** (teacher' name) Mr. Arnold,

Thank you for inviting me to come speak at **(2)** (school name) ______________________.
I am busy flying through **(3)** (state name) ______________________ and will not be able to speak to your class about being a pilot. However, I would like to meet the students and tell them about my job. I will be visiting **(4)** (city name) ______________________ on **(5)** (month name) ______________________ 12.
I would like to invite you to come to the **(6)** (airport name) ______________________ to take a tour. Then I can show the students the inside of a real airplane.

Sincerely,
(7) (name) ______________________

Name ______________________________ Date ______________

Singular and Plural Nouns

A **noun** is a word that names a person, a place, or a thing. Some nouns name only one person, place, or thing. These words are called **singular nouns**. Some words name more than one person, place, or thing. These words are called **plural nouns**. Plural nouns end in **-s**.

Examples: Singular nouns: A chicken is a kind of bird.

Plural nouns: Like most birds, chickens have feathers on their bodies.

Directions: Read the sentences. Circle the word that correctly completes each sentence. Write if the noun is **singular** or **plural**.

1. A chicken has two (wing, wings) that help it fly short distances.

____

2. Unlike most birds, a chicken has a comb that grows on its (head, heads).

____

3. A chicken eats with its pointed (beak, beaks). ______________

4. It eats (bug, bugs) it finds along the ground. ______________

5. A chicken builds a (nest, nests) to sleep in. ______________

6. A hen will lay (egg, eggs) in the nest nearly every day. ______________

Name ______________________ Date ______________

Singular and Plural Nouns

Singular nouns name one person, place, or thing. **Plural nouns** name more than one person, place, or thing. Many plural nouns end in **-s**.

Directions: Read the story. Look at the underlined words. Write each word on the lines to tell if it is **singular** or **plural**.

The Chicken and the Alligator

A chicken perched by the river. Just then, a crocodile snapped at her and caught her wing. "Oh, let me go!" cried the chicken. "You would not want to hurt your sister would you?"

The crocodile paused. "We are not sisters," she said. "I have scales and you have feathers."

"We are sisters," said the chicken. "I will prove it to you."

A few days later, the chicken traded several of her eggs for crocodile eggs when the crocodile was asleep. Soon the eggs hatched.

The crocodile looked in chicken's nest and saw little green babies with scales. "How cute!" she exclaimed. Then she looked at the eggs in her nest. "Oh my, fuzzy animals with beaks," she cried. "I guess we are sisters."

Plural Nouns	Singular Nouns
______________	______________
______________	______________

Name ______________________________ Date ______________

Plural Nouns

Plural nouns name more than one person, place, or thing. Most plural nouns end in **-s**. Words ending in **-s**, **-x**, **-ch**, or **-sh** are made plural by adding **-es**. In nouns that end in **-y**, change the **y** to **i** and add **-es**.

Examples: <u>Cities</u> are busy places.
<u>Buses</u> carry people all over town.

Directions: Read the sentences. Write the correct plural form of each word in parentheses ( ) to complete the sentence.

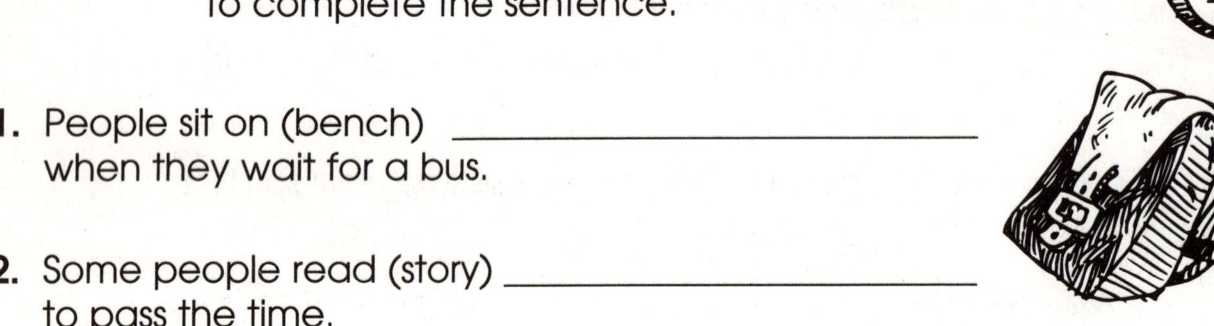

1. People sit on (bench) ______________________ when they wait for a bus.

2. Some people read (story) ______________________ to pass the time.

3. Others carry small (box) ______________________ of things they bought.

4. Many (family) ______________________ ride the bus together.

5. The bus ride can put little (baby) ______________________ to sleep.

6. Some (class) ______________________ ride a bus if they take a field trip.

7. These students might even eat their (lunch) ______________ on the bus.

8. They are always careful to pick up their trash (bag) ______________ when they are done.

Name ______________________________ Date ______________________

Plural Nouns

Plural nouns name more than one person, place, or thing. Most plural nouns end in **-s**. Words ending in **-s**, **-x**, **-ch**, or **-sh** are made plural by adding **-es**. In nouns that end in **-y**, change the **y** to **i** and add **-es**.

Directions: Read the paragraph. Write the plural form of each word in ( ) to complete the sentences.

Leaving the City

Marco watched his mother pack. She had just finished wrapping all the **(1)** (dish) ____________________ in newspaper. Now she was reaching up to get the **(2)** (glass) ____________________ out of the cabinet. "Would you get more wooden **(3)** (box) ____________________ from the living room?" she asked.

"Sure, Mom," Marco said sadly. Mrs. Carlos looked up at the sound of his voice. "What's wrong?" she asked.

"I don't want to move," Marco said. "I like the city."

Mrs. Carlos sighed. "I know you like the city, but there are many different things to do in the country. We can walk in the woods. You can hear birds singing in the tree **(4)** (branch) ____________________ and see rabbits hiding under **(5)** (bush) ____________________. You might even see several **(6)** (fox) ____________________."

"It all sounds good," said Marco. "But I won't have all of my **(7)** (friend) ____________________ to play with."

"It will be hard at first," said Mrs. Carlos. "But school will start soon, and you will make lots of new friends."

"I hope so," said Marco.

Name ______________________________ Date ______________

Possessive Nouns

A **possessive noun** shows ownership. To show possession, add **'s** to words that are singular nouns. Add an apostrophe **(')** to plural nouns that end in **-s**. Add **'s** to plural nouns that do not end in **-s**.

Examples:

Singular noun:	The sun's light shone on the playground.
Plural noun:	The puppies' barks made people look.
Plural noun:	The children's laughter was loud.

Directions: Read the sentences. Write an apostrophe **(')** where it is needed in each sentence.

1. A line formed by the slides ladder.

2. The boys bikes were parked in the rack.

3. The children looked up when they heard the womens calls.

4. A mother hushed her babys cry.

5. The teams cheers sounded when they made a goal.

6. The two girls hands were dirty from the sand.

7. A boys ball rolled under a bench.

8. The ice cream made the childrens hands sticky.

Name ______________________________ Date ____________________

Possessive Nouns

A **possessive noun** shows ownership. To show possession, add **'s** to words that are singular nouns. Add an apostrophe **(')** to plural nouns that end in **-s**. Add **'s** to plural nouns that do not end in **-s**.

Directions: Read the story. Write the possessive form of each word in ( ) to complete the sentences.

The Race

Soon-Lei and Gina raced through the **(1)** (playground) ____________________ gate. The **(2)** (girls) ____________________ skates rolled noisily down the sidewalk. The **(3)** (people) ____________________ stares didn't bother the girls as they raced on. They didn't even hear the two **(4)** (puppies) ____________________ barks.

Soon-Lei pulled ahead slightly as the girls skated to the ice cream stand. Gina could hear Soon-Lei's laughter. "It looks like you're buying today," Soon-Lei called.

"No way!" answered Gina. "I bought the ice cream yesterday!" **(5)** (Gina) ____________________ feet flew faster. Her **(6)** (friends) ____________________ cheers and shouts pushed her on. "I can do this! I can do this!" Gina repeated to herself.

All of a sudden, Gina shot forward and passed Soon-Lei. **(7)** (Gina) ____________________ hand touched the building first. The **(8)** (girls) ____________________ breath sounded loud as they gasped for air.

"Good race," said Soon-Lei. "I guess I am buying the ice cream today."

0-7424-1857-X *Grammar Basics Plus*

Name ______________________ Date ______________

What Is a Verb?

Action words tell what people and things do. Action words are called **verbs**. Add **-s** to most verbs that tell about one person or thing. No ending is added to verbs that tell about more than one person.

Examples: One thing: A crab <u>digs</u> in the sand.
More than one thing: All crabs <u>dig</u> small holes.

Directions: Read the sentences. Circle the verb that correctly completes each sentence.

1. Crabs (crawl, crawls) on the beach at night.
2. They (swim, swims) in shallow water, too.
3. A crab (eat, eats) small plants most often.
4. A crab (look, looks) for small fish to eat.
5. A crab (shed, sheds) its shell as it gets bigger.
6. It (grow, grows) a new shell then.
7. All crabs (hide, hides) while they shed their shell.
8. Without a hard shell to protect the crab, other animals might (eat, eats) it.

Name ______________________________ Date ______________

What Is a Verb?

Action words are called **verbs**. Add **-s** to most verbs that tell about one person or thing. No ending is added to verbs that tell about more than one person.

Directions: Read the story. Write verbs from the box to complete the sentences.

crush	gives	bite	battle	serves	fights	crawls	send

The First Step

Hercules was a strong and wise man in Greek myths. For 12 years, Hercules **(1)** ____________ a king. The king **(2)** ____________ Hercules a task each year that he must complete successfully. Some of the tasks **(3)** ____________ Hercules on journeys into faraway lands. During one task, Hercules **(4)** ____________ a monster that has many heads. The two of them **(5)** ____________ near a swamp. A giant crab **(6)** ____________ out of the muddy waters and uses its claws to **(7)** ____________ Hercules' toe. Hercules does not feel the pinch and steps on the crab. His feet **(8)** ____________ the animal to death. Hera, the goddess of life, thinks the crab was very brave and gives it a place of honor in the sky as one of the constellations, or star patterns.

Name ______________________________ Date ______________

Verbs

Action words are called **verbs**. Add **-s** to most verbs that tell about one person or thing. No ending is added to verbs that tell about more than one person.

Examples: One thing: An elephant breathes with its trunk.

More than one thing: Elephants also use their trunks to pick up food from the ground.

Directions: Read the sentences. Circle the verb that correctly completes each sentence.

1. An elephant (eat, eats) up to 500 pounds of plants each day.
2. Elephants (walk, walks) about 4 miles per hour.
3. These large animals (like, likes) to swim.
4. An elephant (swim, swims) for long distances.
5. It (hold, holds) its trunk up out of the water.
6. The water (help, helps) the elephant stay cool.
7. If there is no water nearby, elephants (flap, flaps) their ears.
8. This motion also (cool, cools) them down.

0-7424-1857-X *Grammar Basics Plus*

Name ______________________________ Date ______________________

Verbs

Action words are called **verbs**. Add **-s** to most verbs that tell about one person or thing. No ending is added to verbs that tell about more than one person.

Directions: Read the story. Write verbs from the box to complete the sentences. Use each word one time only.

play	asks	lifts	return	walk	crawls

The Elephant and the Squirrel

One day, the elephant **(1)** ________________ the little squirrel to go for a swim. The squirrel has never been in the water, but he agrees to try it.

The elephant **(2)** ________________ the squirrel onto his back, and the two friends **(3)** ________________ to the river. Once he is in the water, the elephant leaves the squirrel and swims to the other side of the river. The squirrel does not know how to swim. When the squirrel reaches the bank, he **(4)** ________________ out of the water panting. The squirrel is very tired and sad. The two quietly **(5)** ________________ home.

The next day, the elephant visits the squirrel. "What shall we play today?" asks the elephant.

The little squirrel answers, "I do not want to play with you anymore. We like to **(6)** ________________ different things. What is fun for you hurts me." The elephant was sad to lose his friend. But he realized that not everyone likes the same things.

Name ______________________________ Date ______________________

Linking Verbs

Linking verbs do not show action. These verbs join, or link, the subject to another word in the sentence. The word describes the subject or gives the subject another name. Some linking verbs are **am**, **is**, **are**, **was**, and **were**.

Example: George Washington was our first President.

Directions: Read the sentences. Circle the linking verb in each sentence.

1. Abraham Lincoln was our sixteenth president.
2. Washington and Lincoln were important American men.
3. Washington was the man who helped America gain its freedom from England.
4. Lincoln was the leader during the Civil War.
5. Both presidents were born in February.
6. They are the reason President's Day happens in February.
7. Presidents' Day is the third Monday in February each year.
8. It is the day we remember all presidents.

Name ______________________________ Date ______________

Linking Verbs

Linking verbs do not show action. These verbs join, or link, the subject to another word in the sentence. The word describes the subject or gives the subject another name. Some linking verbs are **am**, **is**, **are**, **was**, and **were**.

Directions: Read the story. Write a linking verb from above to complete the sentences correctly.

George Washington and the Cherry Tree

There **(1)** ______________ a story about George Washington that many students learn. It tells about a time long ago when Washington **(2)** ______________ a young boy. The story says that Washington got an ax and chopped down a cherry tree. Washington's parents asked him if he **(3)** ______________ the person who cut down the tree. Washington did not lie. He said that he **(4)** ______________ the guilty person. His parents **(5)** ______________ not angry because Washington had told the truth.

Today, some people think the story **(6)** ______________ not true. I **(7)** ______________ not sure what to believe. I know my parents would be very angry if I cut down a tree. What do you think?

Name ______________________________ Date ______________

Helping Verbs

A verb shows action. Some verbs have more than one word. These verbs are called **verb phrases**. The most important verb is the **main verb**. A **helping verb** is in front of the main verb. It helps the main verb tell about the action. Some helping verbs are **am**, **is**, **are**, **was**, **were**, **can**, **did**, **have**, **has**, **had**, and **will**.

Example: In the 1800s, many pioneers were going west.

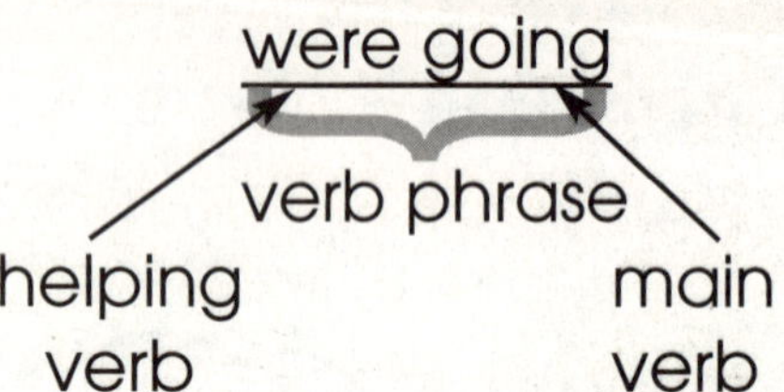

Directions: Read the sentences. Underline the verb phrase in each sentence. Write the helping verb on the line.

1. Pioneers had lived in cities. ______________________

2. They were working long hours. ______________________

3. Many families did dream about farming. ______________________

4. Each family was worried about the trip. ______________________

5. It was going to be difficult. ______________________

6. They had planned the trip carefully. ______________________

7. Today, we have found many letters about the trip. ______________________

8. We always will remember this time in history. ______________________

Name ____________________ Date ____________________

Helping Verbs

Verb phrases are made with two or more verbs. The most important verb is the **main verb**. A helping verb is in front of the main verb. Some helping verbs are **am**, **is**, **are**, **was**, **were**, **can**, **have**, **has**, **had**, and **will**.

Directions: Read the story. Circle the helping verb that completes each sentence correctly.

Elliot **(1)** (was, were) tired of the dirt and the constant bumping of the wagon. He wanted the trip to be over. He and his family **(2)** (has, had) left Independence, Missouri, almost two months ago. They **(3)** (will, were) still on the trail heading west to California.

"I **(4)** (am, had) going to walk for a while," yelled Elliot. He jumped out of the wagon and ran up to the oxen. He **(5)** (were, was) walking beside them when his mother called. "Elliot, **(6)** (did, will) you gather some sticks as you walk?" she asked. "We **(7)** (will, were) stop soon to start a fire for dinner," she said.

Elliot looked along the rocky trail. "There **(8)** (is, are) a pile of brush a little farther ahead," called Elliot. "I **(9)** (are, am) going to run ahead to get it." His mother smiled and waved. Elliot dashed off.

Name ______________________________ Date ______________

The Verb Be (Am, Is, and Are)

The word **be** is a verb. It has different forms. Some forms of **be** are **am**, **is**, and **are**. Use **am** with the word **I**. Use **is** when the subject is one person, place, or thing. Use **are** when the subject is more than one or with the word **you**.

Examples: A crow is a large, black bird.
Most crows are about 21 inches long.

Directions: Read the sentences. Circle the correct verb form of **be** in each sentence.

1. Crows (is, are) not songbirds.
2. Their calls (is, are) loud when a predator comes near.
3. Insects (is, are) a crow's favorite food.
4. Corn (is, are) another favorite food.
5. A farmer (is, are) unhappy when a group of crows flies nearby.
6. The crows (is, are) probably hungry.
7. They (is, are) likely to get into the corn crop.
8. It (is, are) a good idea for the farmer to make a scarecrow.

Name ______________________ Date ______________

The Verb Be (Am, Is, and Are)

The word **be** is a verb. It has different forms. Some forms of **be** are **am**, **is**, and **are**. Use **am** with the word **I**. Use **is** when the subject is one person, place, or thing. Use **are** when the subject is more than one or with the word **you**.

Directions: Read the story. Write a form of the verb **be** to complete the sentences.

The Fox and the Crow

A crow found a piece of cheese and flew into a tree to enjoy the treat. A fox saw the bird and walked to the tree.

"Good morning, Crow!" he called. "How lovely you **(1)** ______________ today! Your feathers **(2)** ______________ so shiny. Your beak **(3)** ______________ such a beautiful shade of yellow. I bet your voice **(4)** ______________ lovely, too. Would you sing for me?"

The crow believed everything she heard. She spread her wings and opened her beak to sing. Immediately, the cheese fell to the ground. The fox grabbed the cheese and swallowed it.

As the fox walked away, he said, "I **(5)** ______________ so glad to have met you! But I will give you some advice. Do not trust people who give you lots of praise. They **(6)** ______________ not to be trusted."

0-7424-1857-X *Grammar Basics Plus*

Name ______________________ Date ______________

The Verb Be (Was and Were)

The word **be** is a verb. It has different forms. Some forms of **be** are **was** and **were**. They tell about the past. Use **was** when the subject is one person, place, or thing. Use **were** when the subject is more than one or with the word **you**. Forms of **be** are used as linking verbs and as helping verbs.

Examples: George Washington Carver was a scientist.
His experiments were done with peanut plants.

Directions: Read the sentences. Circle the verb form of **be** in each sentence.

1. Carver was trying to help the farmers in the South.
2. The soil was poor.
3. The crops were not healthy.
4. It was important to plant peanuts.
5. They were good for the soil.
6. Carver also was the person who invented over 300 peanut recipes.
7. Peanuts were baked in cookies and cakes.
8. Peanuts were even put in a party punch!

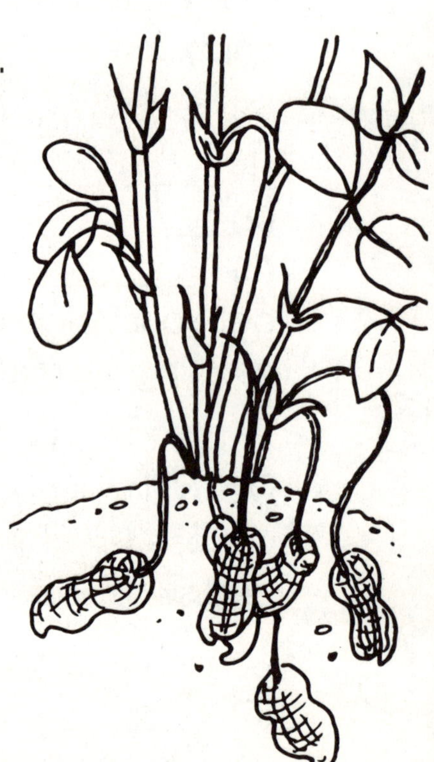

0-7424-1857-X *Grammar Basics Plus*

Name ______________________________ Date ____________________

The Verb Be (Was and Were)

The word **be** is a verb. It has different forms. Some forms of **be** are **was** and **were**. They tell about the past. Use **was** when the subject is one person, place, or thing. Use **were** when the subject is more than one or with the word **you**.

Directions: Read the story. Write **was** or **were** to complete the sentences.

The Nut Jar

A jar **(1)** ____________ filled with nuts. The nuts **(2)** ____________ very big. A boy saw them and wanted some to eat. He put his hand into the jar and grabbed as many as he could. He tried to pull his hand out, but his hand **(3)** ____________ too full. His fist **(4)** ____________ too big to fit through the opening of the jar. The boy began to cry.

Some people **(5)** ____________ watching the boy. One of the women spoke to the boy. She said, "If you **(6)** ____________ less greedy, you would not be having trouble. If you let some of the nuts go, your hand will fit through the jar opening. It is better to have half of something than to have nothing at all."

0-7424-1857-X *Grammar Basics Plus*

Name ______________________ Date ______________

Present Tense Verbs

Action words are called **verbs**. Verbs can tell about actions that happen now. These verbs are **present tense verbs**. Add **-s** to most verbs that tell about one person or thing. Add **-es** to verbs that end in **-s**, **-x**, **-ch**, or **-sh**. For verbs that end in **-y**, change the **y** to **i** and add **-es**. No ending is added to verbs that tell about more than one person.

Examples:

One	**More Than One**
An artist paints pictures.	Artists paint pictures.
The artist brushes paint on a canvas.	Artists brush paint on a canvas.

Directions: Read the sentences. Circle the verb that correctly completes each sentence.

1. Each artist (mix, mixes) different colors of paint.
2. The artist (wish, wishes) to find just the right color.
3. Some artists (splash, splashes) paint on the canvas.
4. Others (paint, paints) with lots of detail.
5. They (fuss, fusses) over a shape until it is perfect.
6. The paint slowly (dry, dries) when the painting is done.
7. No one (touch, touches) the wet canvas.
8. Soon, the artists (sell, sells) their paintings.

Name ______________________________ Date ______________

Present Tense Verbs

Present tense verbs tell about actions that happen now. Add **-s** to most verbs that tell about one person or thing. Add **-es** to verbs that end in **-s**, **-x**, **-ch**, or **-sh**. For verbs that end in **-y**, change the **y** to **i** and add -**es**. No ending is added to verbs that tell about more than one person.

Directions: Read the letter. Write a verb from the box to complete the sentences. Use each word one time.

teaches	fusses	watch	matches	try	wants

Dear Maria,

I am very excited about the art class I am taking. A real artist **(1)** ________________ the class. At first, the students carefully **(2)** ________________ everything she does. Then we **(3)** ________________ to copy her work. The teacher **(4)** ________________ at us, though. She wants us to find our own style.

For my first picture, I painted a basket of flowers. I do not think it was very good. I am working on a vase of flowers now. It **(5)** ________________ my first painting, so I will have a set. Mother really **(6)** ________________ to hang both pictures in the hallway. I will be quite proud of them.

Talk to you soon!

Your friend,
Dana

0-7424-1857-X *Grammar Basics Plus*

Name ______________________ Date ______________

Past Tense Verbs

Action words are called **verbs**. Verbs can tell about actions that happened in the past. These verbs are **past tense verbs.** Add **-d** or **-ed** to most verbs that tell about an action that happened in the past.

Examples: The ancient Greeks enjoyed sports.
They started the Olympic Games.

Directions: Read each sentence. Look at the verb in parentheses ( ). Write the word to show past tense.

1. The Olympic Games (honor) ______________ the Greek gods.
2. People from all over the land (gather) ______________ in Athens, Greece.
3. Men (race) ______________ in the very first Olympic Games.
4. Soon, the Greeks (add) ______________ more events.
5. In one event, two men (box) ______________.
6. In another event, horses (pull) ______________ a carriage.
7. Everyone (cheer) ______________ for the winners.
8. The games (last) ______________ for five days.

Name ______________________________ Date ______________

Past Tense Verbs

Past tense verbs tell about actions that happened in the past. Add **-d** or **-ed** to most verbs that tell about an action that happened in the past.

Directions: Read the story. Write a verb from the box to complete the sentences. Use each word one time.

talked	walked	laughed	curled	decided	crossed

The Tortoise and the Hare

Some animals gathered in the woods one day. The hare **(1)** ______________ about being the best runner. He challenged the other animals to a race to prove his speed.

"I'll race you," said a shy voice.

Everyone looked down at the little green tortoise. The hare **(2)** ______________ out loud at such a silly idea, but he agreed to the race. The two animals **(3)** ______________ to run through the woods and back again.

At the start of the race, the hare hopped quickly down the path. The little tortoise **(4)** ______________ slowly. Soon, the hare was far ahead of the tortoise. He found a spot and **(5)** ______________ up to take a nap in the sun. In the meantime, the tortoise walked on and on. Finally, the hare heard a crowd cheering. The hare woke up just before the tortoise **(6)** ______________ the finish line. The hare leaped up and ran to catch the tortoise, but it was too late! The tortoise had won the race.

Name ______________________ Date ______________

Future Tense Verbs

A **verb** can tell about actions that will happen in the future. These verbs are **future tense verbs**. Future tense verbs use the helping verb **will** with a main verb.

Example: Each American will throw away about 3.6 pounds of garbage every day.

Directions: Read the sentences. Underline the future verb in each sentence.

1. Americans will toss 50 billion cans in one year.
2. They also will dump 27 billion glass bottles into the trash.
3. Nearly 87 percent of our garbage will go to a landfill.
4. It will take nearly 400 years for some things to break down.
5. Many Americans will recycle to help.
6. They will reuse food bags and boxes.
7. They will find new uses for things, too.
8. Many people will reduce the trash that goes to a landfill.

Name ______________________________ Date ______________

Future Tense Verbs

Future tense verbs can tell about actions that will happen in the future. They use the helping verb **will** with a main verb.

Directions: Read the poem. Write the future tense form of the verb in parentheses ( ) to complete the sentences.

Helping Earth

Our Earth is in trouble—I know this is true.

There is pollution in the air and in the water, too.

Our landfills are filling up with bottles and cans,

But in this world are a number of Earth fans.

They **(1)** (find) ____________________ a way to make our Earth new.

I plan to join them—here is what I **(2)** (do) ____________.

I **(3)** (reuse) ____________________ my lunch bag at school.

I **(4)** (ride) ____________ my bike so the car won't use fuel.

I **(5)** (recycle) ____________________ my newspapers and cans.

I **(6)** (wash) ____________________ by hand the dishes and pans.

Things like these are quite simple to do.

Won't you join me and help our Earth, too?

Name ______________________ Date ______________

Verb Agreement

The subject of a sentence must agree in number with the verb. A **singular** subject means there is one person, place, or thing. A singular subject goes with a singular verb. A **plural** subject means there is more than one person, place, or thing. A plural subject goes with a plural verb.

Examples: Singular: A seed grows inside most flowers.

subject verb

Plural: Seeds grow inside most flowers.

Directions: Read the sentences. Circle the verb that correctly completes each sentence. Write **singular** or **plural** to show the number of the subject and verb.

1. Most seeds (drop, drops) beside the plant. ______________
2. But some seeds (travel, travels) to new places. ______________
3. A seed (move, moves) in several different ways. ______________
4. They (catch, catches) a ride on the fur of animals. ______________
5. The wind (blow, blows) some seeds to new places. ______________
6. Small animals also (carry, carries) the seeds away. ______________
7. The seed (fall, falls) on the ground. ______________
8. Soon, a new plant (grow, grows) roots. ______________

Name ______________________________ Date ______________________

Verb Agreement

The subject of a sentence must agree in number with the verb. A **singular subject** goes with a singular verb. A **plural subject** goes with a plural verb.

Directions: Read the story. Write a verb from the box to complete the sentences.

runs	grow	look	follows	stick	climb

A Seedy Dog

Keiko and his dog Cody walked out of the woods and back home.

Mrs. Basura looked out the door. "How was your walk?" she asked.

"Every time we go in the woods, Cody **(1)** __________________ through the tall grass," said Keiko. "All those seeds with hooks **(2)** __________________ to his coat. It will take hours to brush them off."

Mrs. Basura laughed. "Cody is probably chasing the squirrels. The squirrels **(3)** __________________ for acorns on the ground. They **(4)** __________________ into the trees when they hear Cody. Cody **(5)** __________________ them through the grass to the trees."

"He does have fun," sighed Keiko.

"Please put the seeds in the trash," said Mrs. Basura. "Those seeds **(6)** __________________ into weeds quickly."

"I will," answered Keiko. "I do not want to pull weeds from the yard. Getting them off the dog is bad enough!"

Name ______________________ Date ______________

Irregular Verbs

Some verbs do not add **-ed** to show the past tense. The word spelling changes and is very different from the present tense. These kinds of verbs are called **irregular verbs**.

Present	Past
leave	left
bring	brought
come	came

Examples: Present: People still come to America today.
Past: Many people came to America long ago.

Directions: Read the sentences. Circle the verb that correctly completes each sentence.

1. The people (leave, left) their homes looking for a new life.

2. They (know, knew) there would be danger.

3. The people (take, took) a chance because they wanted freedom.

4. They (write, wrote) letters telling about their lives in a new land.

5. Today, many people (begin, began) new lives in the United States.

6. They can (come, came) by airplane or ship or even by walking.

7. Some people today (bring, brought) very little with them.

8. They try to (make, made) a new life by working hard.

Name ______________________ Date ______________

Irregular Verbs

Some verbs do not add **-ed** to show the past tense. The word spelling changes and is very different from the present tense. These kinds of verbs are called **irregular verbs**.

Directions: Read the letter. Write a verb from the box to complete the sentences.

go	met	thought	began	went	run

Dear Huang,

We arrived in the United States two weeks ago. I (1) ____________ school two days later. I was very scared at first. I (2) ____________ it would be hard to make new friends. Boy, was I wrong! I (3) ____________ two new friends immediately.

My new friends are John and Charles. They were going to play soccer after school and asked me to join them. I (4) ____________ with them to the park. They were surprised because I was able to score a goal when I was out in the field. They asked me to join their soccer team!

Now, I (5) ____________ to soccer practice three times a week. We (6) ____________ sprints and practice dribbling the ball. My first game is this weekend. I am really excited about it. I will write another letter next week to tell you about the game.

At first, I was sad when we moved away from Korea. But it is really fun here. I miss all of my school friends, though. Tell everyone I said hello.

Yours truly,
Kwan

Name ______________________ Date ______________

What Is a Pronoun?

A **pronoun** is a word that takes the place of one or more nouns. Some pronouns are **I**, **you**, **he**, **she**, **it**, **we**, and **they**. These pronouns take the place of nouns in a sentence.

Example: A commercial tries to get people to buy something.
It tries to get people to buy something.

Directions: Read the sentences. Look at the pronouns listed above. Choose a pronoun to take the place of the underlined word or words in each sentence. Write the pronoun on the line.

1. Many commercials are on television. ______________
2. An actress may tell you how great something is. ______________
3. An actor may show you how to use something. ______________
4. Baseball players even make commercials. ______________
5. The commercial makes something look fun. ______________
6. Television viewers need to be careful. ______________
7. Remember that the people on television get paid. ______________
8. Only buy something if you will use it. ______________

Name ______________________________ Date ______________

What Is a Pronoun?

A **pronoun** is a word that takes the place of one or more nouns. Some pronouns are **I**, **you**, **he**, **she**, **it**, **we**, and **they**. These pronouns take the place of nouns in a sentence.

Directions: Read the advertisement. Write a pronoun to take the place of the word or words in parentheses ( ).

Hello folks out there in television land! My name is Ima Star, and this is my dog, Ben. **(1)** (Ben and I) ____________ want to tell you all about a new dog food called Tasty. **(2)** (Tasty) ____________ is Ben's favorite food. I do not need to call Ben when it is time for dinner. **(3)** (Ben) ____________ hears me scoop the food from the bag. Ben comes running because he loves the taste of **(4)** (Tasty) ____________ so much!

You see, the people who make Tasty know dogs. **(5)** (The people who make Tasty) ____________ know what a dog loves to eat. **(6)** (The people who make Tasty) ____________ also know what a dog needs to be healthy and happy. Don't **(7)** (the viewer) ____________ want a healthy dog, too? Then you should buy Tasty because **(8)** (Tasty) ____________ is the best!

Name ______________________________ Date ______________

Subject and Object Pronouns

A **pronoun** is a word that takes the place of one or more nouns. Some pronouns take the place of nouns in the subject of a sentence. These pronouns are called **subject pronouns**. Some subject pronouns are **I**, **you**, **he**, **she**, **it**, **we**, and **they**. Some pronouns take the place of nouns that follow an action verb or the words **to**, **at**, **for**, and **with**. These pronouns are called object pronouns. Some **object pronouns** are **me**, **you**, **him**, **her**, **it**, **us**, and **them**.

Example: Jane Goodall studies monkeys.

Subject pronoun: She studies monkeys.
Object pronoun: Jane Goodall studies them.

Directions: Read the sentences. Choose a pronoun to take the place of the underlined word or words in each sentence. Write the pronoun on the line.

1. Jane Goodall is a famous scientist. ______________
2. When Jane was young, she went to Africa to watch monkeys. ______________
3. At first, the monkeys were very shy. ______________
4. Soon, the monkeys got used to seeing Jane. ______________
5. Jane gave names to the monkeys. ______________
6. She called one male monkey David Greybeard. ______________

Name ______________________________ Date ______________________

Subject and Object Pronouns

Subject pronouns take the place of nouns in the subject of a sentence. Some subject pronouns are **I**, **you**, **he**, **she**, **it**, **we**, and **they**. **Object pronouns** take the place of nouns that follow an action verb or the words **to**, **at**, **for**, and **with**. Some object pronouns are **me**, **you**, **him**, **her**, **it**, **us**, and **them**.

Directions: Read the story. Choose a pronoun from the lists above to take the place of the word or words in parentheses ( ). Write the pronoun on the line to complete the sentences.

The Monkey and the Crab

A monkey saw a crab carrying some rice. The monkey called out, "Crab, **(1)** (This monkey) ____________ have a persimmon seed. I will happily trade **(2)** (the seed) ____________ for your rice."

The crab agreed. The monkey climbed to the ground and gobbled up the rice. He threw the seed to **(3)** (the crab) ____________. "You did not make a wise choice," he said. **(4)** (The crab) ____________ smiled. She took the seed to a field and buried it.

Later that year, the crab came looking for the monkey. "Big persimmons are growing on my tree, but **(5)** (the persimmons) ____________ are too high for me to reach. You may have some if you will throw one to me."

The monkey climbed into the tree and began eating the persimmons. Then **(6)** (the monkey) ____________ chased the crab to her hole. The monkey put his tail inside and poked at the crab. **(7)** (The crab) ____________ pinched the monkey's tail. She refused to let go until the monkey behaved himself. The monkey finally agreed. They shared the persimmons between **(8)** (the crab and the monkey) ____________.

Name ______________________________ Date ______________

Possessive Pronouns

A **pronoun** is a word that takes the place of one or more nouns. Some pronouns tell who or what owns something. These pronouns are called **possessive pronouns**. Some possessive pronouns are **my**, **your**, **his**, **her**, **its**, and **their**.

Example: Cardinals are birds that have a crest of feathers on <u>their</u> heads.

Directions: Read the sentences. Circle the possessive pronoun in each sentence.

1. A male cardinal has bright red feathers on his body.
2. A female cardinal has darker feathers on her body.
3. A cardinal uses bark to make its nest.
4. Their favorite foods are ants and berries.
5. Both the male and the female take care of their babies.
6. One baby bird always has its mouth open.
7. You can use your binoculars to watch the birds.
8. You can read my book to learn more about cardinals.

0-7424-1857-X *Grammar Basics Plus*

Name ______________________________ Date ____________________

Possessive Pronouns

Possessive pronouns tell who or what owns something. Some possessive pronouns are **my**, **your**, **his**, **her**, **its**, and **their**.

Directions: Read the story. Write a possessive pronoun from the list above to complete the sentences.

How the Redbird Became Red

Raccoon saw Wolf resting by a tree. He raced up to Wolf and pulled **(1)** ____________ tail, then raced away quickly. Raccoon scampered up a tree and looked down from the safety of **(2)** ____________ branches.

Wolf stopped under the tree. He did not see **(3)** ____________ tricky friend. Wolf leaned against the tree. **(4)** ____________ cool shade made him feel better. Soon, he fell asleep.

Raccoon climbed down from the tree. He thought of another trick to play on Wolf. Raccoon scooped up some mud and spread it on Wolf's eyes.

When Wolf woke up, **(5)** ____________ eyes were sealed shut. "Help!" he cried. "Someone help me!"

A small brown bird flew down to Wolf. "What can I do to help you?" she asked.

"Please get this stuff off of **(6)** ____________ eyes," said Wolf.

The bird used **(7)** ____________ beak to carefully peck away the mud. Before long, Wolf could see. "I would like to thank you," said Wolf. He used red rocks to paint the little bird with spots of bright red. Since then, all cardinals are proud of **(8)** ____________ red feathers.

Name ____________________ Date ____________________

Demonstrative Pronouns

Demonstrative pronouns point out people, places, and things. The demonstrative pronouns are **this, that, these,** and **those**.

Example: This is a snowboard.

Directions: Read the sentences. Circle the demonstrative pronoun in each sentence.

1. That tall, snowy mountain is good for snowboarding.
2. Those are the lifts up to the peak of the mountain.
3. These are the people who like to snowboard.
4. Snowboarders balance on the board like this.
5. If you like skiing, you should definitely try this!
6. I don't think I could do that right away.
7. Beginners practice snowboarding on small hills like those.
8. You will need some goggles, so take these.

Name ____ Date ________________________

Demonstrative Pronouns

Demonstrative pronouns point out people, places, and things. The demonstrative pronouns are **this, that, these,** and **those.**

Directions: Read the sports interview. Write a possessive pronoun from the list above to complete the sentences.

Announcer: Thanks for joining us at beautiful Mountain Ridge. **(1)** ____________ is a great day for the snowboard freestyle event. I would like to introduce you to Albert Brown. He is ahead of everyone right now.

Albert: Thanks for having me here.

Announcer: **(2)** ____________ mountains are very steep. What is it like to ski on them?

Albert: Most of the mountains are really fun. There is one difficult mountain called "The Master." **(3)** ____________ is one mountain that takes hard work to learn.

Announcer: Who are the people over there in the audience?

Albert: **(4)** ____________ are my friends. They always come along to cheer for me.

Announcer: We wish you luck, Albert. To show our thanks, we'd like to give you some new goggles.

Albert: Thank you. I will definitely use **(5)** ____________.

Name ______________________________ Date ______________

Interrogative Pronouns

Interrogative pronouns are words used at the beginning of asking sentences, or questions. The interrogative pronouns are **who, whose, whom, what**, and **which**.

Example: What do you want to know about my friend's birthday party?

Directions: Read the sentences. Circle the interrogative pronoun in each sentence.

1. On which day will you celebrate your birthday?
2. Whose idea was it to have a party?
3. Who is sending the invitations?
4. What time does the party start?
5. Whom did you invite to the party?
6. Who will be attending the celebration?
7. To whom should I address my reply?
8. What time will the party end?

0-7424-1857-X *Grammar Basics Plus*

Name ______________________________ Date ______________________

Interrogative Pronouns

Interrogative pronouns are words used at the beginning of questions. The interrogative pronouns are **who**, **whose**, **whom**, **what**, and **which**.

Directions: Read the poem. Write an interrogative pronoun from the list above in parentheses ( ) to complete the sentences.

Birthday Plans

Planning a party is usually fun.
There are many decisions to make.
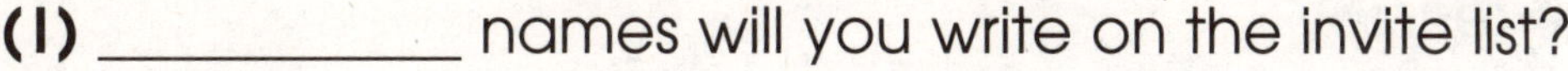
(1) ____________ names will you write on the invite list?
(2) ____________ flavor will you choose for the cake?
(3) ____________ do you think will be able to come,
And **(4)** ____________ day will you celebrate?
(5) ____________ should you call to ask for help
When you are ready to decorate?
Planning a party is usually fun.
But these decisions are too hard to make.
It might be easier to ask one friend
To join you for a day at the lake!

Name ______________________________ Date ______________

Antecedents

A **pronoun** takes the place of a noun. Some pronouns are **I**, **you**, **he**, **she**, **it**, **we**, **you**, and **they**. Most often, a pronoun renames a noun in the same sentence or in the sentence before. The noun that the pronoun renames is called the **antecedent**.

Example: Chewing gum was first discovered in Mexico. It is made from the resin of a tree.

antecedent — pronoun

Directions: Read the sentences. Underline the pronoun in each pair of sentences. Then circle the antecedent.

1. Some Americans were traveling in Mexico.
They saw the resin.

2. The resin seeped from cuts on the tree.
It got hard when exposed to the air.

3. William Wrigley was one of the Americans.
He and his friends had an idea.

4. The Americans shipped blocks of resin to the United States.
They designed machines that shaped the resin into small balls of gum.

5. Eventually, the gum was formed into strips.
It was flavored, too.

6. Traveling salesmen sold the gum.
They said the gum was healthy.

Name ______________________ Date ______________

Antecedents

Pronouns are words that take the place of a noun. Some pronouns are **I**, **you**, **he**, **she**, **it**, **we**, **you**, and **they**. Most often, a pronoun renames a noun in the same sentence or in the sentence before. The noun that the pronoun renames is called the **antecedent**.

Directions: Read the story. Look at each underlined pronoun. Circle its antecedent.

Tina had practiced blowing bubbles all month. **(1)** <u>She</u> was getting ready for the Super Duper Big Bubble Blowing Blast. Tina wanted to win the contest. Every day after school, Tina chewed five pieces of bubble gum all at once. Then, when the gum had the right texture, she took a deep breath and blew. The bubble got to be about 12 inches around, but Tina knew **(2)** <u>it</u> wasn't big enough.

Today, Tina decided to try six pieces of gum. Her best friend Beth watched. "**(3)** <u>I</u> think you should use at least nine pieces of gum," said Beth. "Last year, Tyler won the contest. **(4)** <u>He</u> used eight pieces."

Tina stuffed six pieces of gum into her mouth. She chewed for a while and blew again. The bubble got so large that Tina had to cross her eyes to look at **(5)** <u>it</u>.

"Wow!" gasped Beth. "That is a really big bubble. It has to be at least 18 inches across. Try blowing just a little more air into the bubble."

Tina slowly blew a bit more air. POP! Tina was suddenly covered with pink sticky gum.

Beth laughed, "I don't like that shade of pink. **(6)** <u>It</u> is definitely not your color!"

Name ______________________________ Date ______________

What Is an Adjective?

Adjectives are words that describe people, places, and things. Adjectives give more information about **what kind**, **which one**, or **how many**.

Examples: A lion is <u>one</u> kind of big cat.
A lion's fur is <u>brown</u>.
The <u>male</u> lion has a <u>huge</u> mane around its neck.

Directions: Read the sentences. Underline the adjective in each sentence.

1. A lion's roar can be heard five miles away.
2. Up to 35 lions live in groups called "prides."
3. The female lions are the hunters.
4. They look for prey that is old.
5. A lion can eat up to 40 pounds of meat.
6. After eating, lions are lazy.
7. Lion cubs are small.
8. Brown spots cover their fur.

Name ______________________________ Date ______________

What Is an Adjective?

Adjectives are words that describe people, places, and things. Adjectives give more information about **what kind**, **which one**, or **how many**.

Directions: Read the story. Write an adjective from the box to complete the sentences. Use word clues to choose the correct word.

strong	green	greatest	five	one	long

The Lioness

Some animals sat in a field. They were arguing about which animal had the **(1)** ______________ number of babies.

"I lay hundreds of eggs," said a **(2)** ______________ frog. "I surely have the most babies."

"I have up to **(3)** ______________ babies," said a rabbit with **(4)** ______________ ears. "But I have babies several times each year!"

A lioness walked by the animals. She stopped to listen to them talk.

"How many babies do you have?" asked a deer.

"I only have three or four babies," answered the lioness. "But please remember that **(5)** ______________ of my babies will become the animal king. He will be a **(6)** ______________ ruler. The value of an animal is not in the number, but in what he does."

Name ______________________________ Date ____________________

Adjectives That Compare

Adjectives are words that describe people, places, and things. Some adjectives compare nouns. Add **-er** to most adjectives to compare two people, places, and things. Add **-est** to most adjectives to compare three or more people, places, and things. Use the words **more** and **most** when the adjectives have more than one syllable.

Examples: An Olympic runner is <u>fast</u>.
A house cat is <u>faster</u> than the Olympic runner.
The cheetah is the <u>fastest</u> runner of all animals.

Directions: Read the sentences. Underline the adjective in each sentence.

1. A shark is a big fish.
2. A blue whale is bigger than a shark.
3. A whale shark is the biggest fish of all.
4. A scared dog is ferocious.
5. A hungry lion is more ferocious than a dog.
6. The piranha fish is the most ferocious animal.
7. A proboscis monkey is funny looking.
8. Which animal do you think is the funniest looking?

Name ______________________________ Date ________________

Adjectives That Compare

Adjectives can compare nouns. Add **-er** to most adjectives to compare two people, places, and things. Add **-est** to most adjectives to compare three or more people, places, and things. Use the words **more** and **most** when the adjectives have more than one syllable.

Directions: Read the story. Circle the adjective in parentheses ( ) that correctly completes the sentences.

Monkey Talk

The students from West Hill School were visiting the zoo. Mr. Chung, a zookeeper, was giving the students a tour. The tour stopped at the monkey house.

"Monkeys are some of the **(1)** (more intelligent, most intelligent) animals," Mr. Chung said. "They make sounds to talk with each other."

"Is a mandrill **(2)** (larger, largest) than an ape?" asked one student.

"Monkeys and apes are different kinds of animals," answered Mr. Chung. "Most monkeys have a tail. Monkeys are also **(3)** (faster, fastest) runners. Apes are **(4)** (better, best) climbers than monkeys. The ape is **(5)** (bigger, biggest) than a mandrill. But the mandrill is the **(6)** (bigger, biggest) monkey of all."

All of a sudden, one monkey began leaping and screaming loudly. The students laughed as they watched.

"We call that monkey Charlie," said Mr. Chung. "He is the **(7)** (louder, loudest) monkey we have."

"I think he is the **(8)** (funnier, funniest) one, too!" said one of the students.

Name ______________________________ Date ____________________

Adverbs

Adverbs are words that describe verbs. Adverbs tell **where**, **when**, or **how**. Most adverbs end in **-ly**.

Examples: The dark clouds gathered quickly over the water.
There would be a thunderstorm soon.

Directions: Read the sentences. Underline the adverb in each sentence.

1. The clouds moved swiftly toward the land.
2. Suddenly, lightning streaked from a cloud.
3. The thunder crashed loudly.
4. Then people ran to find shelter.

5. They were safely inside when the rain began to fall.
6. It poured heavily for over an hour.
7. The sun came out later that afternoon.
8. It shone brightly in the sky for the rest of the day.

Name ______________________________ Date ____________________

Adverbs

Adverbs describe verbs. Adverbs tell **where**, **when**, or **how**. Most adverbs end in **-ly**.

Directions: Read the letter. Write an adverb from the box to complete the sentences.

suddenly	Lately	swiftly	today	dangerously	Soon

Dear Nate,

We get to do all kinds of different activities at camp. **(1)** ____________________, I have become interested in sailing. It is quite an adventure to skim **(2)** ____________________ across the water.

I did get a scare **(3)** ____________________ when John and I went sailing after breakfast this morning. We did not know there were storm warnings when we took the boat out. We were sailing smoothly across the water when the wind changed direction **(4)** ____________________. The wind became very gusty and just about knocked the boat over. John and I were **(5)** ____________________ close to falling into the water. **(6)** ____________________, dark clouds appeared over us. We raced back to the boat dock. I think I will check the weather forecast before going out in the sailboat from now on.

Your friend,
Jared

Name ______________________________ Date ______________

Use Good and Well

The words **good** and **well** are often confused. **Good** is an adjective. It means "something is better than average." **Well** is an adverb. It means "something was done in a good way."

Examples: It is important to eat food that is good for you.
Eating the right food will make you feel well.

Directions: Read the sentences. Circle the word that correctly completes each sentence.

1. It is a (good, well) idea to learn about different foods.
2. A (good, well) diet makes you healthy.
3. You will perform (good, well) in school.
4. You will get (good, well) grades.
5. You will do (good, well) in your sports events, too.
6. You might surprise yourself with how (good, well) you do.
7. You may think that healthy foods do not taste as (good, well) as sweets.
8. But many foods taste (good, well) and are also (good, well) for you.

Name ______________________________ Date ______________

Use Good and Well

The words **good** and **well** are often used incorrectly. **Good** is an adjective. It means "something is better than average." **Well** is an adverb. It means "something was done is a good way."

Directions: Read the story. Write **good** or **well** to complete the sentences.

A Good Game

"I want to do **(1)** __________ in the baseball tournament next week," Alex told his mother. "But I have been having trouble batting lately."

"Your friend Jana is a **(2)** __________ batter," said Mrs. Smith. "Could you ask her to give you some help?"

"That's a **(3)** __________ idea!" exclaimed Alex. "She always bats **(4)** __________."

"I also think you should try to eat better, too," continued Mrs. Smith. "All that soda and candy is not **(5)** __________ for you. Eating **(6)** __________ will help you be a **(7)** __________ athlete."

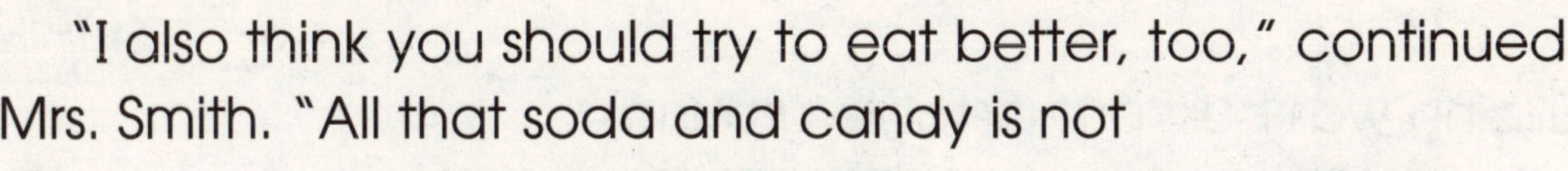

"I like your first idea better," said Alex. "But I know that eating **(8)** __________ food, such as fruits and vegetables, is important, too. I will try."

"I think you will find that your entire game will improve greatly," said Mrs. Smith.

Name ______________________________ Date ______________

Prepositions

A **preposition** shows how some words in a sentence are related. There are many prepositions.

about	behind	from	onto
above	below	in	over
after	between	into	through
at	down	off	to
before	for	on	with

Examples: The Leaning Tower is in Pisa, Italy.
The building leans to one side.

Directions: Read the sentences. Underline the preposition in each sentence.

1. The Leaning Tower was started in 1173.

2. The tower was completed between 1360 and 1370.

3. When three stories were built, the tower started leaning to the side.

4. The building was built on unstable ground.

5. The tower was closed for repair.

6. Engineers straightened it about 15 inches.

7. The tower is now open to visitors.

8. From the seventh floor, it now leans nearly 14 feet.

Name ______________________________ Date ____________________

Prepositions

A **preposition** shows how some words in a sentence are related. Some prepositions are **as**, **around**, **before**, **between**, **by**, **for**, **from**, **in**, **of**, **on**, **over**, **to**, **up**, and **with**.

Directions: Read the postcard. Write prepositions that will correctly complete the sentences.

Dear Aunt Kim,

Mom and I got to Italy two days ago. We have already been (1) __________ many interesting sights. My favorite place so far has been the Leaning Tower. It was built (2) __________ 200 years ago and was used (3) __________ a bell tower. It is famous because it leans to one side.

The tower is made (4) __________ marble. It also has many arches (5) __________ the outside. The tower has 300 stairs inside. We climbed all the way to the top (6) __________ the tower. We were very tired once we got there, but we were glad we did it. The view (7) __________ the top was beautiful! I am sending this card (8) __________ you to see the Leaning Tower. You would really like it.

Your nephew,
Will

Name ______________________________ Date ______________

Conjunctions

A **conjunction** is a word that joins words or groups of words. The words **and**, **or**, and **but** are conjunctions. Use **and** to show that two things are joined. Use **or** to show a choice between two things. Use **but** to show that two things are different.

Examples: You can see the moon <u>and</u> stars at night.
You can view stars with your eyes <u>or</u> with a telescope.
The stars shine during the day, <u>but</u> you cannot see them.

Directions: Read the sentences. Underline the conjunction in each sentence.

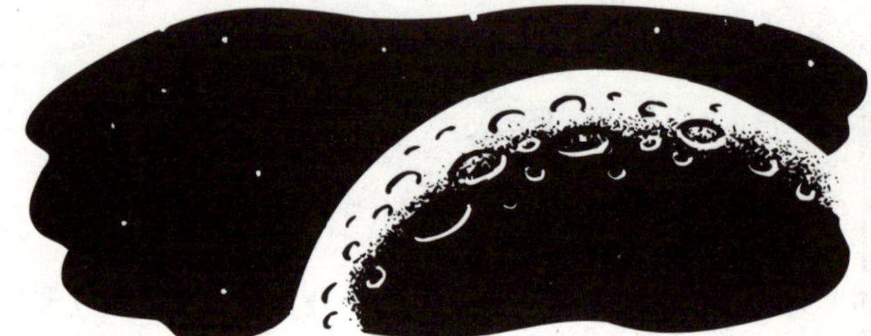

1. Stars give off heat and light because they are made of hot gases.
2. Stars differ in brightness because of their size or their distance from Earth.
3. Stars are really bright, but they seem dim because they are far away.
4. The sun is a star, but it looks bigger because it is close to Earth.
5. Some stars form pictures or patterns in the sky.
6. Ancient people named the star patterns, but everyone knows the names now.
7. Two names are The Big Dipper and the Great Bear.
8. You can read a book or look on the Internet to learn more about stars.

Name ______________________________ Date ______________

Conjunctions

A **conjunction** is a word that joins words or groups of words. The words **and**, **or**, and **but** are conjunctions. Use **and** to show that two things are joined. Use **or** to show a choice between two things. Use **but** to show that two things are different.

Directions: Read the story. Write **and**, **or**, or **but** to complete the sentences.

A giant lion roamed the roads **(1)** ____________ hills of a nearby town. The people in the city could not walk around town **(2)** ____________ visit people on neighboring farms. Many people tried to catch the lion, **(3)** ____________ no one had been able to do so.

A mighty king asked Hercules for help. Hercules was both wise **(4)** ____________ brave. Hercules set out to find the lion. When Hercules and the lion met, there was a huge battle. Hercules tried to use a club, **(5)** ____________ the wood shattered. Next, Hercules tried to shoot his arrows, **(6)** ____________ they bounced off the lion's fur. Finally, Hercules grabbed the lion **(7)** ____________ squeezed its neck. The lion did not bother people **(8)** ____________ other animals again.

Name ______________________________ Date ____________

Simple and Complex Sentences

Some sentences tell about one idea. These sentences are called **simple sentences**. Sometimes, two simple sentences tell about the same idea. They can be joined together to make a longer sentence. These sentences are called **complex sentences**. A **conjunction** is a word that joins complex sentences. The words **and**, **or**, and **but** are conjunctions.

Example: Apples grow on trees. Oranges grow on trees.
Apples <u>and</u> oranges grow on trees.

Directions: Read the sentences. Join the sentences to make complex sentences.

1. Apples can be red. Apples can be green.

____

2. Oranges are sweet. Oranges are juicy.

____

3. People eat the skin of apples. People do not eat the skin of oranges.

____

4. Apples are a fruit. Oranges are a fruit.

____

Name ______________________________ Date ____________________

Simple and Complex Sentences

Simple sentences tell about one idea. These sentences can be joined together to make a longer sentence. These sentences are called **complex sentences**. A **conjunction** is a word that joins complex sentences. The words **and**, **or**, and **but** are conjunctions.

Directions: Read the story. Write **and**, **or**, or **but** to complete the sentences.

Atlanta's Race

Atlanta was a strong **(1)** ___________ swift runner. She could beat any woman **(2)** ___________ man in a foot race. Atlanta's father decided that she should marry. Atlanta did not want to marry, **(3)** ___________ she could not disagree with her father. So, Atlanta came up with a plan. She would only marry a man who could beat her in a running race.

Melanion had loved Atlanta for a long time, **(4)** ___________ he knew he could not beat her in a race. So Melanion visited the goddess Aphrodite. She gave Melanion three golden apples **(5)** ___________ helped him make a plan to win the race.

At the start of the race, Melanion dropped one apple. Atlanta stopped to pick it up. Just as Atlanta came close to Melanion again, he dropped another apple. Atlanta stopped to pick it up, **(6)** ___________ she ran more quickly to catch up. As Melanion **(7)** ___________ Atlanta got close to the finish line, Melanion dropped the last apple. Atlanta picked this apple up, too, **(8)** ___________ this time, she was unable to catch up. Melanion won the race. Atlanta was pleased. While Melanion was not a swift runner, he was very smart.

Name ______________________________ Date ______________

Interjections

An **interjection** is a word that expresses strong feelings, such as anger or joy. These words are usually found at the beginning of a sentence. They are followed by an exclamation mark **(!)** or a comma **(,)**. Some interjections are **oops, wow, whew, oh, aha**, and **gee**.

Examples: Wow! The mall is really crowded today.
Gee, shopping for shoes may take a long time.

Directions: Read the sentences. Underline the interjection in each sentence.

1. Great! This store does not have these shoes in my size.
2. Ouch! These shoes are too little.
3. Oops! Don't run into the person walking in front of you.
4. Oh, I like the shoes in that store window.
5. Aha! I found some shoes I like.
6. Whew! They found shoes in my size.
7. Yay! All my shopping is done.
8. Hurray! We can go home now.

Name ______________________________ Date ______________________

Interjections

An **interjection** is a word that expresses strong feelings, such as anger or joy. These words are usually found at the beginning of a sentence. They are followed by an exclamation mark **(!)** or a comma **(,)**. Some interjections are **oops**, **wow**, **whew**, **oh**, **aha**, and **gee**.

Directions: Read the story. Write an interjection from the box to complete the sentences.

Yikes	Gee	Great	Wow	Oh	Aha

Bike Money

"**(1)** ____________! Look at this cool bike," said Ricardo. "I would love to have a bike like this."

Ian looked closely at the magazine picture. "**(2)** ____________! That is a cool bike! How much does it cost?"

"It costs over $100. **(3)** ____________! That's a lot of money," said Ricardo.

"Do you have any money saved?" asked Ian.

"**(4)** ____________, yes!" answered Ricardo. "I have saved my allowance for over a month now. I have about $30."

"**(5)** ____________! I have an idea," shouted Ian. "Why don't you mow lawns or baby-sit for your neighbors? The Johnsons always call my sister, and she doesn't have time to help because she has a job in a store."

"**(6)** ____________! I will give the Johnsons a call," said Ricardo. "It should not take long to earn the money."

0-7424-1857-X *Grammar Basics Plus*

Name ______________________ Date ______________

Unit 1 Assessment

Directions: Read the sentences. Look at each underlined word. Write its part of speech on the line.

Parts of Speech

noun	pronoun
verb	adverb
adjective	preposition
conjunction	interjection

1. Most people enjoy sunny weather.

____

2. They can go outside to play.

____

3. But the weather can change quickly. ______________________

4. Dark clouds build in the sky and form thunderstorms. ______________

5. Thunder and lightning fill the sky. ______________________

6. In some parts of the United States, tornadoes may form. ______________

7. Have you ever seen the damage from a tornado? ______________

8. Wow! Tornadoes can flatten houses and trees. ______________

Name ______________________________ Date ______________

Unit 1 Assessment

Directions: Read the story. Circle the words that correctly complete the sentences.

Pecos Bill Rides a Tornado

Pecos Bill was a famous cowboy. **(1)** (He, She) could ride anything that moved. One day, Bill decided that he wanted to ride a **(2)** (tornado, tornadoes). It couldn't be just any tornado, either. It had to be the **(3)** (bigger, biggest) one of all. So, Bill waited and waited.

After a while, the sky turned black **(4)** (and, or) gray. The wind tore a tree out of the ground. Old Bill **(5)** (sit, sat) quietly and waited for the tornado to come close. As the tornado whipped past, Bill grabbed it and jumped on. **(6)** (Wow, Great)! That tornado was really angry. It swirled and hissed as it tried to get Bill **(7)** (on, off) its back. Bill just held on **(8)** (more, most) tightly. Every now and then, Bill poked the tornado with **(9)** (their, his) spurs.

The tornado headed to California. It **(10)** (pours, poured) rain all along the way. In fact, it rained so hard that it washed out the Grand Canyon. Finally, there was no rain left. The wind died out, too. Bill fell off and hit the ground so hard that it sank below sea level. **(11)** (Today, Yesterday), folks call the area Death Valley.

Many people heard about Bill's wild ride. They thought it sounded like fun. They were all too **(12)** (scared, happy) to ride tornadoes, though. So, they decided to ride bulls. And that is how the rodeo got started!

Name ______________________________ Date ______________

Subject and Verb Agreement

The subject of a sentence is what the sentence is about. The subject must **agree** in number with the verb, or action word. A singular noun goes with a singular verb. A plural noun goes with a plural verb.

Examples: Singular noun and verb: The ocean rises twice each day .
Plural noun and verb: Oceans rise twice each day.

Directions: Read the sentences. Circle the noun in each sentence. Underline the verb. Then, write if the noun is **singular** or **plural**.

1. The ocean falls again, too. ______________________

2. Treasures lay on the beach after high tide.

____

3. Often, people walk along the beach. ______________________

4. The people hunt for seashells and interesting rocks.

____

5. A child picks up any shell that looks pretty. ______________________

6. Most people look for special shells. ______________________

7. A lucky person finds a starfish. ______________________

8. All beach visitors stay away from living crabs that pinch.

____

Name ______________________ Date ______________

Subject and Verb Agreement

The subject of a sentence must **agree** in number with the verb. A singular noun goes with a singular verb. A plural noun goes with a plural verb.

Directions: Circle the verb that correctly completes the sentences.

A Starfish Story

Ellie and Mary were walking along the beach. All of a sudden, Ellie exclaimed, "Look, Mary, a starfish!" Both girls stopped to look at the spiny sea animal.

"Wow! Look at all those tubes on its arms," said Ellie.

"Those tubes **(1)** (help, helps) the starfish walk. All starfish **(2)** (use, uses) those tubes to eat, too."

"How does it eat?" asked Ellie.

"Starfish **(3)** (like, likes) to eat clams," said Mary. "They **(4)** (grab, grabs) the outside of the shell and pull it open."

"How can a tiny starfish eat a huge clam?" asked Ellie.

"Actually, a starfish **(5)** (push, pushes) its stomach outside of its body through that little hole," said Mary. "The stomach **(6)** (move, moves) inside the clam shell, and juices from the stomach dissolve the clam."

"Wow! I didn't know starfish **(7)** (was, were) so interesting!" exclaimed Ellie.

"This starfish **(8)** (appear, appears) to be alive yet," Mary said. "Let's put it back in the ocean."

Name ______________________________ Date ______________

Verb Tense

Past tense verbs tell about actions that happened in the past. Add **-ed** to most verbs to form the past tense. **Present tense** verbs tell about actions that happen now. Add **-s** or **-es** to most verbs to go with a singular subject. Do not add anything to the verb for a plural subject. **Future tense** verbs tell about actions that will happen later. The helping verb **will** is added before most verbs to make the future tense.

Examples:

Past tense:	Long ago, people lived in caves.
Present tense:	Today, many people live in stone and wooden buildings.
Future tense:	In the future, people will live in buildings on the moon.

Directions: Read the sentences. Circle the verb in each sentence. Write if the verb is **past**, **present**, or **future** tense.

1. American settlers stacked logs to make cabins. ______________

2. Long ago, fires warmed these homes. ______________

3. Today, an architect designs homes. ______________

4. Some kinds of houses can even move on wheels. ______________

5. Many years from now, homes will be different. ______________

6. People will build homes on the moon. ______________

Name ______________________ Date ______________

Verb Tense

Past tense verbs tell about actions that happened in the past. Add **-ed** to most verbs to form the past tense. **Present tense** verbs tell about actions that happen now. Add **-s** or **-es** to most verbs to go with a singular subject. Do not add anything to the verb for a plural subject. **Future tense** verbs tell about actions that will happen later. The helping verb **will** is added before most verbs to make the future tense.

Directions: Read the letter. Write a verb from the box to complete the sentences.

join	want	settled	will play	planted	will eat

Dear Neighbors,

As you know, we (1) ______________ in this town over a year ago. We built a log cabin and (2) ______________ crops in the fields. It has been a hard first year as settlers. But the harvest was good.

Now that we are settled, we (3) ______________ to build the barn. Please (4) ______________ us on Saturday for the traditional barn-raising party. Once the frame is built, we (5) ______________ dinner. Then we (6) ______________ games and sing songs. It will be lots of fun, as all of you know.

Your neighbor,
John Moore

Name ______________________ Date ______________

Irregular Verbs

Some verbs do not add **-ed** to show the past tense. The word spelling changes and is very different from the present tense. These kinds of verbs are called **irregular verbs**.

Present Tense	**Past Tense**
buy	bought
say	said
go	went

Examples: Present tense: Many people buy tickets for baseball games.
Past tense: Many of these people bought tickets last year, too.

Directions: Read the sentences. Circle the irregular verb in each sentence. Write if the verb is **present** or **past** tense.

1. The players began their practice in the spring. ______________

2. They went to camp to work with the coaches. ______________

3. The team won games early in the season. ______________

4. The fans saw how well the team played. ______________

5. Now all of the games sell out. ______________

6. During the game, the pitcher throws the ball to the batter. ______________

7. The batter swings the bat. ______________

8. Players in the outfield catch the ball. ______________

Name ______________________ Date ______________

Irregular Verbs

Some verbs do not add **-ed** to show the past tense. The word spelling changes and is very different from the present tense. These kinds of verbs are called **irregular verbs**.

Directions: Read the sports newscast. Circle the verb that correctly completes the sentences. Then write each verb in the column to tell if it is **present** or **past tense**.

Game-Time Announcing

Hello, sports fans! This is Lou Downs with WMHP, your sporting radio station. This game has been very exciting. Ben Lewis **(1)** (catch, caught) two fly balls in the third inning. He also **(2)** (get, got) three hits so far. He **(3)** (run, ran) to third base on one of those hits. Because of Ben Lewis, the Tigers are leading by two points.

We are beginning the third inning now. Lewis **(4)** (comes, came) to the plate. The fans **(5)** (see, saw) Lewis, and they are going wild. Here comes the pitch. Lewis **(6)** (swings, swung). The ball **(7)** (flies, flew) up in the air. Wow! Lewis just hit a home run. That player is amazing. You just won't **(8)** (find, found) a better baseball player!

Present	**Past**
____________	____________
____________	____________
____________	____________
____________	
____________	

Name ______________________________ Date ______________

Pronouns and Antecedents

Pronouns are words that take the place of a noun. Some pronouns are **I**, **you**, **he**, **she**, **it**, **we**, and **they**. Most often, a pronoun renames a noun in the same sentence or in the sentence before. The noun the pronoun renames is called the **antecedent**.

Example: antecedent ⟶ Many people worked for freedom in the American Revolution.

pronoun ⟶ They worked for freedom in the American Revolution.

Directions: Read the sentences. Rewrite each sentence using a pronoun.

1. The Americans wanted to be free from British rule.

____

2. George Washington led the American soldiers.

____

3. The soldiers fought the British.

____

4. Betsy Ross sewed the first American flag.

____

5. You and I have freedom because of those brave Americans.

____

Name ______________________________ Date ______________________

Pronouns and Antecedents

Most often, a pronoun renames a noun in the same sentence or in the sentence before. Some pronouns are **I, you, he, she, it, we,** and **they**. The noun the pronoun renames is called the **antecedent**.

Directions: Read the story. Look at each underlined pronoun. Circle the antecedent of each underlined word.

The American Flag

Many Americans know the name Betsy Ross. **(1)** <u>They</u> learned about Betsy Ross in history class. **(2)** <u>She</u> was the woman who designed and sewed the very first American flag. The story says that George Washington went to Betsy's house. **(3)** <u>He</u> asked her to sew the flag. George and Betsy talked about what the flag should look like. **(4)** <u>They</u> decided that the flag should be red, white, and blue. **(5)** <u>It</u> would have 13 stars set in a circle on a field of blue. Each star would represent a colony in the United States.

The American flag has changed over the years. **(6)** <u>It</u> now has 50 stars because there are 50 states. You and I should be proud of what Betsy Ross did. **(7)** <u>We</u> still enjoy seeing that flag today.

Name ______________________________ Date ______________

Prefixes

A **prefix** is a word part added to the beginning of a word to change its meaning.

Prefix	Meaning	Word
mis-	wrong, not, badly	misunderstand
pre-	before	prepay
re-	again, back	redo
un-	opposite of	unclear

Example: Computers are unbelievable machines. (not believable)

Directions: Read the sentences. In each sentence, circle the word that has the prefix. Then write the meaning of each circled word.

1. You might be uncertain how to spell a word.

____

2. The computer can check to see which words are misspelled.

____

3. Then you can retype the word.

____

4. It is very easy to undo most mistakes you make on a computer.

____

5. You can also preview a page before printing to make sure it looks right.

____

Name ____ Date ____________________

Prefixes

A **prefix** is a word part added to the beginning of a word to change its meaning.

Directions: Read the story. Write a word from the box to complete the sentences. Use each word one time only.

rejoin	unhappy	dislike	preview	unable	misuse	unusual	rewrite

Keisha stood in front of Mr. Morgan's desk. She was very **(1)** ____________________ with her grade.

"This grade is **(2)** ____________________ for you," said Mr. Morgan. "Why don't you **(3)** ____________________ the paper? Then I will check it and record the better grade."

Keisha sighed in relief. "Thank you, Mr. Morgan," she said. "I will bring it back to school on Monday."

As Keisha walked away, she thought about her weekend. Keisha would need to call her friends and tell them she was **(4)** ____________________ to go on the camping trip they had planned. She didn't want them to **(5)** ____________________ her for backing out. Luckily, Keisha had typed the paper on a computer. She could **(6)** ____________________ her changes on the screen before she printed the paper. Then, maybe her father could take her to the park Saturday morning to **(7)** ____________________ her friends.

"Thank goodness for computers," thought Keisha. "They sure save a lot of extra work!" But just to make sure she didn't **(8)** ____________________ her time, Keisha planned to begin the paper as soon as she got home from school.

Name ______________________________ Date ______________

Suffixes

A **suffix** is a word part added to the end of a word to change its meaning.

Prefix	**Meaning**	**Word**
-er	one who	farmer
-ful	full of	successful
-less	without, not able to	hopeless
-ly	in that way	swiftly

Example: Parades are enjoyable events. (able to be enjoyed)

Directions: Read the sentences. Circle the word that has the suffix in each sentence. Then write the meaning of each circled word.

1. Bands play their instruments loudly.

____

2. The marchers keep rhythm as they step.

____

3. The people on the floats wave happily.

____

4. They are careful to hold onto the rails.

____

5. They do not want to be careless and fall off the float.

____

Name ______________________________ Date ______________

Suffixes

A **suffix** is a word part added to the end of a word to change its meaning.

Directions: Read the story. Replace the words in parentheses ( ) with a word from the box that has the same meaning.

speechless	loudly	careless	countless	happily	leader	colorful

The Best Band

Our school band was marching in a parade. All of us had spent **(1)** (without count) ________________ hours practicing the music and marching at school. Now, we were actually marching down a street in front of a crowd. After all our work, we didn't want to be **(2)** (without care) ________________. The band **(3)** (one who leads) ________________ marched in front to direct us. We watched her closely. We played the music **(4)** (in a loud way) ________________ for everyone to hear. The color guard twirled **(5)** (full of color) ________________ flags. The crowd cheered **(6)** (in a happy way) ________________ as we marched past. After the parade, we were **(7)** (without speech) ________________ when we got the award for the best band.

Name ______________________ Date ______________

Synonyms

A **synonym** is a word that has the same meaning or almost the same meaning as another word.

Example: A long time ago, there were several tribes of Iroquois.
A long time ago, there were several groups of Iroquois.

Directions: Read the sentences. Then read the words in parentheses ( ) at the end of each sentence. Circle the word that is a synonym for the underlined word.

1. The different Iroquois tribes fought among themselves. (argued, played)
2. One chief wanted to stop the fighting. (law, leader)
3. He wanted them to join together. (desired, asked)
4. Then all of the tribes could live quietly together. (angrily, peacefully)
5. The chief spoke calmly to each tribe. (yelled, talked)
6. They agreed to form a league of tribes. (join, destroy)
7. Afterwards, the people led happy lives. (contented, active)
8. They had found a way to live together. (ignored, discovered)

Name ______________________ Date ______________

Synonyms

A **synonym** is a word that has the same meaning or almost the same meaning as another word.

Directions: Read the story. Replace each word in parentheses ( ) with a word from the box that has the same meaning.

bundle	sons	strength	attempted	break	divided

The Bundle of Sticks

A father had several **(1)** (boys) ____________ who always argued among themselves. The father **(2)** (tried) ____________ to teach the boys how to get along, but they continued to fight. Then one day, the father called his sons together and showed them a **(3)** (group) ____________ of sticks. He asked each boy to **(4)** (snap) ____________ the group in half. Each son tried with all his **(5)** (might) ____________, but the sticks could not be broken. Then, the father gave each boy one stick to break. The sticks broke quite easily.

"If you all work together, you will be strong like the group of sticks," said the father. "But if you are **(6)** (separated) ____________ among yourselves, you will be easily broken like the one stick. Remember, there is strength in numbers."

Name ______________________________ Date ______________

Antonyms

An **antonym** is a word that has the opposite meaning of another word.

Example: The wolf is one of the smallest animals in the dog family.
The wolf is one of the largest animals in the dog family.

Directions: Read the sentences. Then read the words in parentheses ( ) at the end of each sentence. Circle the word that is an antonym for the underlined word.

1. A wolf has a poor sense of smell. (great, short)

2. Wolves live alone in groups. (single, together)

3. One wolf is the follower in the group. (joiner, leader)

4. This wolf holds its tail down in the air. (up, under)

5. Wolves howl quietly at night. (softly, loudly)

6. When wolves hunt, they look for healthy prey. (sick, growing)

7. They run slowly after the animal they are chasing. (quickly, noisily)

8. Most people think wolves are friendly. (safe, dangerous)

Name ________________________________ Date ____________________

Antonyms

An **antonym** is a word that has the opposite meaning of another word.

Directions: Read the story. Replace each word in parentheses ( ) with a word from the box that has the opposite meaning.

top	funny	quickly	come	angrily	up

The Boy Who Cried Wolf

A boy had a job guarding sheep. One day, he thought it would be **(1)** (serious) ____________________ to play a trick on the people in the village. The boy ran **(2)** (slowly) ____________________ down the hill crying loudly, "Wolf! Wolf!"

The people in the village ran **(3)** (down) ____________________ the hill to help. When they got to the **(4)** (bottom) ____________________ of the hill, there was no wolf in sight.

"Don't ever do that again," the people said as they marched **(5)** (happily) ____________________ down the hill.

The next day, the boy played the same trick. The people were angry when they saw they had been tricked again.

On the third day, a wolf did creep into the field. As it began to attack the sheep, the boy called out loudly, "WOLF! WOLF!" The people would not listen to the boy's cries. "That boy is playing another trick," they said.

Finally, the boy ran to his father. "Why did you not **(6)** (leave) ____________________ when I called?" he asked.

"We thought you were playing tricks again," his father said. "You have not told the truth, so no one believed you!"

0-7424-1857-X *Grammar Basics Plus*

Name ______________________ Date ______________

Compound Words

A **compound word** is made when two or more small words are joined together.

Example: There are many things to do in the summertime. (summer + time)

Directions: Read the sentences. Write the two words that make up each underlined compound.

1. People can go for a sailboat ride on the lake.

   ____

2. They can put on a swimsuit and go swimming in the pool.

   ____

3. They roast hot dogs over a campfire.

   ____

4. Some people play baseball in the park.

   ____

5. The park playground is full of busy children, too.

   ____

Name ______________________________ Date ______________________________

Compound Words

A **compound word** is made when two or more small words are joined together.

Directions: Read the story. Write a compound word from the box to complete the sentences.

notebook	treehouse	rainbow	bluebird	butterfly	inchworm

Animal Drawings

Khou sat in his **(1)** ____________________ and watched the activities of the animals around him. He held a **(2)** ____________________ in his hands and was sketching the different animals he saw. Khou began drawing a colorful **(3)** ____________________ that perched in a nearby tree. The bird was busy finding blades of grass and taking them to build a nest.

Next, Khou saw a **(4)** ____________________ float by. Its bright wings looked like a small **(5)** ____________________ with all the colors. Khou wished he had brought his chalks with him so he could get the color patterns just right. It soon danced away into the woods.

Khou was about to get up when he noticed a small **(6)** ____________________ crawling on his paper. Its little body made a hook shape.

"Oh, so you want your picture drawn, too!" Khou exclaimed. He quickly drew the shape of the little insect. "That was too easy! You need to come back later in the summer when you are a moth."

Name ______________________ Date ______________

Homophones

Homophones are words that sound alike but have different spellings and meanings.

Example: Have you ever (scene, seen) a little mouse.

Scene means "a setting."
Seen means "viewed."

Directions: Read the sentences. Circle the homophone that correctly completes each sentence.

1. Look carefully, because you might (see, sea) a mouse scampering in the grass.
2. A mouse has big ears and a long, thin (tale, tail).
3. Mice are usually active at (night, knight).
4. They creep out (two, too, to) search for food.
5. A mouse might eat nuts and (berries, buries).
6. It might nibble on plant (routes, roots), too.
7. This small creature (choose, chews) on many wooden objects.
8. If you are very quiet, you might (here, hear) a mouse in your house.

0-7424-1857-X *Grammar Basics Plus*

Name ______________________________ Date ______________

Homophones

Homophones are words that sound alike but have different spellings and meanings.

Directions: Read the story. Circle the homophone in the parentheses ( ) that correctly completes the sentences.

The Mice and the Cat

(1) (Won, One) day, the mice called a meeting to discuss ways to protect themselves from a cat. They talked for **(2)** (ours, hours) but were unable to **(3)** (find, fined) the perfect plan.

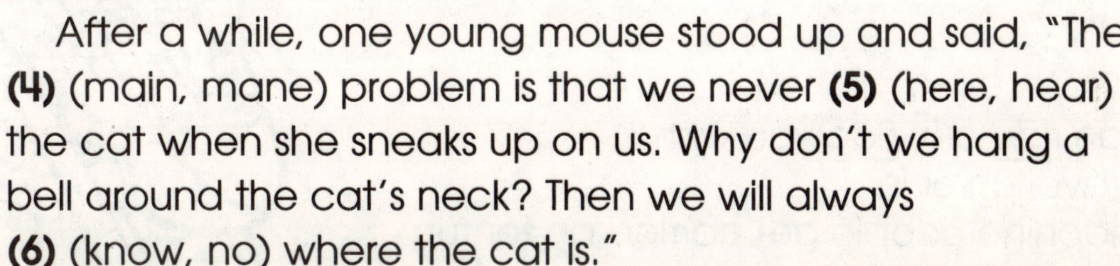

After a while, one young mouse stood up and said, "The **(4)** (main, mane) problem is that we never **(5)** (here, hear) the cat when she sneaks up on us. Why don't we hang a bell around the cat's neck? Then we will always **(6)** (know, no) where the cat is."

All the mice began **(7)** (to, too, two) exclaim at once, "What a perfect plan! We have found a **(8)** (weigh, way) to outsmart that cat at last!"

Then a wise, old mouse stood up and spoke, "The idea of the bell is a good plan. We could **(9)** (hear, here) the bell to learn **(10)** (where, wear) the cat is at all times. But tell me, who will put the bell on the cat?"

All of the mice grew quiet and looked around the room, but no one spoke. The old mouse shook his head and said, "Some things are easier said than done!"

Name ______________________________ Date ______________

Homographs

Homographs are words that are spelled alike but have different meanings. Homographs might even be pronounced differently.

Example:

It is a <u>fair</u> (a) day to go to the <u>fair</u> (b).

a. beautiful
b. a place to show farm goods; a carnival

Directions: Read the sentences and definitions. Write letters by each underlined word to show its meaning.

1. There was a <u>jam</u> of people by the <u>jam</u> contest.
a. a fruity food used on toast and sandwiches
b. crowd

2. You can <u>ride</u> any <u>ride</u> you wish.
a. to travel on or in
b. a machine people get carried on for fun

3. Most people <u>long</u> to go on the roller coaster because it is a <u>long</u> ride.
a. a great amount
b. to wish for

4. <u>Watch</u> your <u>watch</u> so we know when to leave.
a. a tool that keeps time
b. to look at

Name ____________________ Date ____________________

Homographs

Homographs are words that are spelled alike but have different meanings. Homographs might even be pronounced differently.

Directions: Read the definitions. Then read the story. Write definition letters on the lines to show the meaning of each underlined word.

might
- **a.** could, a possibility
- **b.** strength

pet
- **c.** an animal that lives with people
- **d.** to stroke with a hand

second
- **e.** after the first
- **f.** a very short amount of time

Fun at the Fair

There is so much to do at a fair. Children like to visit the baby animals in the farmyard. They can **(1)** pet ____________ the animals as they feed them. Some children even hug an animal as if it were a **(2)** pet ____________. These animals hold still for only a **(3)** second ____________, though, before running off to find more food.

Some people like to play games. A man **(4)** might ____________ want to show how strong he is. He will swing a hammer with all of his **(5)** might ____________ to move a weight up a pole. On his **(6)** second ____________ try, the weight will ring a bell at the top and the man will win a prize.

Whatever kind of fun people like, they can find it at the fair!

Name ____________________ Date ____________________

Troublesome Words

Homophones are words that sound alike but have different spellings and meanings. Homophones can cause spelling problems. Some troublesome homophones are listed below.

To means "toward."
Too means "also."
Two means "the number 2."

Their means "belong to."
They're means "they are."
There means "in that place."

Example: Hummingbirds are able ((to,) two, too) hover in the air.

Directions: Read the sentences. Circle the homophone that correctly completes each sentence.

1. Hummingbirds can fly backwards, (to, two, too).

2. (Their, They're, There) wings beat about 60 to 70 times a second.

3. (Their, They're, There) one of the few birds that can halt in the air.

4. The smallest hummingbird is (to, two, too) inches long.

5. The largest hummingbird grows (to, two, too) over eight inches long.

6. You often see hummingbirds where (their, they're, there) are colorful flowers.

7. They use (their, they're, there) long tongues (to, two, too) drink nectar from inside the flowers.

8. Hummingbirds enjoy eating insects, (to, two, too).

Name ______________________________ Date ______________

Troublesome Words

Homophones are words that sound alike but have different spellings and meanings. Homophones can cause spelling problems. Some troublesome homophones are **their**, **they're**, **there**, and **to**, **too**, **two**.

Directions: Read the story. Write a homophone from the list above to complete the sentences correctly.

The Creation of Hummingbirds

The creator sat in the forest looking at the animals he had made. "**(1)** __________ are no animals in the sky," he thought sadly.

So, creator made an animal with **(2)** __________ wings. He covered the wings with bright feathers so they would be as light as the air. When the creator was done, he smiled. Now **(3)** __________ were animals on the land and in the air, **(4)** __________.

The creator watched the animals again. He saw some leftover feathers. They were bright green, blue, and red. "It would be a shame not to use such beautiful feathers," thought the creator. "I will make another bird. It must be very small because **(5)** __________ are few feathers left."

So, the creator set **(6)** __________ work and made **(7)** __________ small birds. He covered **(8)** __________ wings with the green feathers. He put the blue feathers on **(9)** __________ heads. Finally, he put the red feathers on **(10)** __________ throats. The birds hummed with joy as they flew away.

"**(11)** __________ the most beautiful birds off all!" the creator thought as they flew up **(12)** __________ the sky.

Name ______________________ Date ______________

Contractions

A **contraction** is a word made by joining two words. When the words are put together, one or more letters are left out. An **apostrophe (')** takes the place of the missing letters.

cannot	can't	she would	she'd
I am	I'm	you will	you'll
is not	isn't	will not	won't

Example: The winter is not a good time to plant a garden.
The winter isn't a good time to plant a garden.

Directions: Read the sentences. Look at the underlined words. Rewrite each sentence with a contraction.

1. Most plants will not grow during the winter.

   ____

2. They do not get enough heat to help them grow.

   ____

3. They usually cannot get enough water either.

   ____

4. To grow plants in the winter, you will need a greenhouse.

   ____

5. It is a see-through building where plants stay warm all year long.

   ____

Name ______________________________ Date ______________________________

Contractions

A **contraction** is a word made by joining two words. When the words are put together, one or more letters are left out. An **apostrophe (')** takes the place of the missing letters.

Directions: Read the story. Write the underlined words as contractions on the lines.

Winter Flowers

Maggie looked outside at the piles of snow. The roads were deserted because people **(1)** could not ________________ drive on the slick ice. The trees were bare and lifeless. "**(2)** I am ________________ glad I am in here where **(3)** it is ________________ warm and cheerful," Maggie thought.

Maggie had built a greenhouse last year so her plants and flowers **(4)** would not ________________ die in the winter. Maggie was happy because she had found a wonderful way to use her beautiful plants. She picked the flowers and gave them to people in the neighborhood who **(5)** were not ________________ feeling well.

Maggie's neighbor, Mrs. Keats, had just come home from the hospital. Maggie decided to cut some flowers to take to Mrs. Keats. "**(6)** They will ________________ make Mrs. Keats feel more cheerful," thought Maggie. "They always make me feel better." Maggie got some scissors and carefully cut the flowers that **(7)** she would ________________ take to her neighbor.

Name ______________________________ Date ______________

Double Negatives

The words **but**, **never**, **no**, **not**, **nobody**, **nothing**, **hardly**, and **only** are **negative words**. Contractions with **-n't** are also negatives. A **double negative** is a sentence in which there are two negative words. Two negatives should not be used in the same sentence.

Example: Incorrect: Famous people don't hardly go out in public.
Correct: Famous people don't go out in public.

Directions: Read the sentences. Circle the two negatives in each sentence. Then rewrite each sentence correctly.

1. Famous people, such as movie stars, don't want nobody to recognize them.

____

2. They can't hardly go outside without adoring fans bothering them.

____

3. Once a star is seen, there's nothing nobody can do.

____

4. The star won't go to that place no more.

____

5. They will never again tell nobody where they are going.

____

Name ______________________________ Date ______________

Double Negatives

A **double negative** is a sentence in which there are two negative words. Two negatives should not be used in the same sentence.

Directions: Read the story. Underline the sentences that have double negatives. Rewrite each sentence on the lines below. (Hint: There are six sentences.)

Tamara couldn't hardly believe her luck. Her best friend Lisa had gotten tickets to the Dream Girls concert. Tamara hadn't been allowed to tell nobody, though. "Mother bought only two tickets," Lisa said. "So, I can't take nobody else!" So, Tamara hadn't said nothing. It was hard to keep a secret from all of her friends.

The worst part was that Tamara had gotten an autograph of Jewels, the lead singer. Jewels didn't never give autographs to anyone. "No one wouldn't believe me if I did show the autograph anyway," sighed Tamara. She put the autograph away in her drawer where it was safe.

____

____

____

____

____

____

Name ______________________ Date ______________

Unit 2 Assessment

Directions: Read the sentences. Circle the verb that correctly completes each sentence.

1. People (live, lived) in castles many years ago.
2. These huge buildings (keep, kept) the people safe.
3. Today, people (visit, visited) the castles.
4. As they explore, visitors (will learn, have learned) what life was like long ago.

Directions: Read the sentences. Circle the two negatives in each sentence. Then rewrite the sentence correctly.

5. Visitors can't hardly believe how people lived long ago.

____

6. The people did not have no running water.

____

Directions: Read the sentences. Write a pronoun that can take the place of the underlined word.

7. <u>People</u> long ago did not have refrigerators. ______________
8. <u>A computer</u> is a new invention, too. ______________

Name ______________________________ Date ______________

Unit 2 Assessment

Directions: Read the sentences. Circle the word at the end of the sentence that is a synonym of the underlined word.

1. Jerry walked into the dark, damp castle. (wet, hot)

2. The small windows did not let much light inside. (large, tiny)

Directions: Read the sentences. Circle the word at the end of the sentence that is an antonym of the underlined word.

3. Jerry was excited that he was able to visit such a boring place. (dull, fantastic)

4. He had read few books about knights and castles. (some, many)

Directions: Read the sentences. Circle the word that best completes each sentence.

5. "It would have been fun (to, too, two) be a knight," thought Jerry.

6. Then, Jerry remembered how heavy and hot (their, they're, there) armor was.

Directions: Read the sentences. Circle the word at the end of the sentence that takes the place of the underlined words.

7. Jerry did not like the heat. (disliked, likely)

8. Jerry thought in a happy way about the cool air inside his house. (happy, happily)

Name ______________________________ Date ______________

Sentence Endings

A **sentence** tells what someone or something does or was. All sentences begin with a capital letter. A **declarative** sentence tells about something. It ends in a period **(.)**. An **interrogative** sentence asks a question. It ends in a question mark **(?)**. A **command** gives a direction. It ends in a period **(.)**. An exclamation shows strong feeling. It ends with an **exclamation** point **(!)**.

Examples:

Declarative:	A fox is a member of the dog family.
Interrogative:	Did you know that foxes like to eat chickens?
Command:	Close the gate to the chicken coop.
Exclamation:	There is a fox!

Directions: Read the sentences. Write the correct punctuation mark at the end of each sentence. Write **declarative**, **interrogative**, **command**, or **exclamation** to name the kind of sentence.

1. Foxes hunt for food mostly at night ______________
2. Do you know how they hunt ______________
3. They listen for sounds that a prey might make ______________
4. That fox is standing on its hind legs to see above the grass ______________
5. Don't move or you will scare it away ______________
6. Look how fast that fox can run ______________

Name ____ Date ________________________

Sentence Endings

A **declarative** sentence tells about something. It ends in a period **(.)**. An **interrogative** sentence asks a question. It ends in a question mark **(?)**. A **command** gives a direction. It ends in a period **(.)**. An **exclamation** shows strong feeling. It ends with an exclamation point **(!)**.

Directions: Read the story. Write the correct punctuation mark at the end of the sentences.

The Fox Without a Tail

One day, a fox was hunting near a farm. He did not watch where he was going and got caught in a farmer's trap. The fox wiggled and twisted until he was free of the trap, but he lost his big, bushy tail. The fox was very embarrassed. "What will I do **(1)** _____" he asked.

The fox hid in the woods for several days trying to think of a plan **(2)** _____ Then one day, he had an idea. He trotted to a field where the other foxes had gathered.

The fox called out loudly, "Look at me, friends **(3)** _____ I got rid of my tail **(4)** _____ How wonderful it is to be free of such a big, heavy weight **(5)** _____"

All of the foxes gasped when the saw the fox without his tail. "Don't you think I look great **(6)** _____" the fox continued. "You should do the same so you can look like me."

The oldest fox stood up and spoke, "If you still had your tail, would you ask us to cut off our tails **(7)** _____" he asked. "Go away, young fox **(8)** _____ You are too interested in helping us because you know that misery loves company."

Name ______________________ Date ______________

Commas

A **comma (,)** makes a sentence easier to read. Use a comma before the words **and** and **or** when listing three or more things. Use a comma after the introductory words **first**, **next**, **then**, **last**, and **so**.

Examples: The fly's life cycle is made up of the egg, larva, pupa, and adult stages.

First, the adult fly lays eggs.

Directions: Read the sentences. Write a comma in each sentence where it is needed.

1. The flies lay their eggs on the ground on the water or on other animals.
2. Then the eggs hatch into the larva stage.
3. The larva lives in rotting plants food or garbage.
4. The larva eats grows and builds a cocoon.
5. Next the larva becomes a pupa and changes to look like an adult fly.
6. Finally the adult fly breaks out of the cocoon.

0-7424-1857-X *Grammar Basics Plus*

Name ______________________________ Date ______________

Commas

Use a **comma (,)** before the word **and** when listing three or more things. Use a comma after the introductory words **first**, **next**, **then**, **last**, and **so**.

Directions: Read the story. Write a comma where it is needed. (Hint: You should write 10 commas.)

Fly Saves the River

Long ago there was a beautiful river that flowed through the land. The water was clear cool and clean. Many of the animals came to drink from it.

One day a moose came to drink from the water. The moose was a huge animal and drank large amounts of the water. The water quickly disappeared because the moose came to drink each day.

The animals met to discuss the problem. "What shall we do?" they asked. Moose was so big that all the animals were afraid to talk to him.

Then the fly decided to drive moose away. "I am small," said Fly. "Moose will not see me!" So Fly went to the river the next morning and waited for Moose. When Moose lowered his head to drink, Fly bit him on the leg. Moose stamped his foot hard and left a deep hole that filled with water.

Next Fly bit moose on his hind foot. Moose stamped again, making another hole. Fly continued to bite Moose all over. Moose stamped shook and twisted to get rid of Fly, but nothing worked. Finally Moose ran away from the river and did not return.

"I may be small," said Fly. "But I am very smart!"

Name ____________________ Date ____________

Quotation Marks

A **quote** tells the exact words that a person says. Use **quotations marks (" ")** before and after these words. Use a comma at the end of the quote when the speaker's name is included at the end of the sentence. Use a period at the end of the quote when the speaker's name is at the beginning of the sentence. Always use a question mark or an exclamation point inside the quotation marks if the sentence is a question or an exclamation.

Examples: "The Alaskan brown bear is the largest bear," said the park ranger.
"What is the smallest bear?" asked one person.

Directions: Read the sentences. Circle the quotation marks. Underline the punctuation.

1. "The Malayan bear is the smallest bear," answered the ranger.

2. The ranger said, "This bear is only three to four feet long when it is fully grown."

3. "That is a small bear!" said one girl.

4. Another person asked, "What do bears eat?"

5. "Most bears eat meat, fruits, leaves, and insects," said the ranger.

6. He then said, "Many bears travel long distances to find food."

7. "The polar bear has been known to swim over 200 miles to hunt for seals," the ranger added.

8. "Wow! That's a long way to travel to find food!" said one man.

Name ______________________________ Date ______________

Quotation Marks

A **quote** tells the exact words that a person says. Use **quotations marks (" ")** before and after these words. Use a comma at the end of the quote when the speaker's name is included at the end of the sentence. Use a period at the end of the quote when the speaker's name is at the beginning of the sentence. Always use a question mark or an exclamation point inside the quotation marks if the sentence is a question or an exclamation.

Directions: Read the story. Write the correct punctuation mark in the sentences.

How Bear Lost His Tail

A long time ago, Fox was jealous of Bear's long, bushy tail. So, Fox cut a hole in the icy lake and used a line to catch several big fish. When Bear walked by, Fox stuck his tail in the water.

"Look at all those fish you caught **(1)** _____" exclaimed Bear. "How did you get so many fish **(2)** _____"

Fox smiled and said **(3)** _____ "I used my tail!"

(4) _____ I want to catch fish like that," said Bear.

"Then sit down here on the ice **(5)** _____" said Fox. "Put your tail in the water. I will go hide and tell you when you catch a fish."

Bear sat on the ice and put his long tail in the icy water. Fox walked home. Nighttime came and Fox went to sleep.

"Good morning, Bear! **(6)** _____ shouted Fox the next morning. Bear jumped up at the sound of Fox's voice. SNAP! Bear's beautiful tail broke off.

"Oh, my tail **(7)** _____" Bear cried. "I will get you for this! **(8)** _____ Since that day, bears have had short tails, and they have not been friends with foxes.

Name ______________________ Date ____________

Proper Nouns

A **noun** is a word that names a person, a place, or a thing. A **proper noun** names a special person, place, or thing. All proper nouns begin with capital letters. Some proper nouns are made with more than one word.

Examples:

Person: George Washington lived long ago.
Place: He was born in Virginia.
Thing: He grew up along the banks of the Potomac River.

Directions: Read the sentences. Underline the proper noun or nouns in each sentence.

1. George Washington was born on February 22, 1732.

2. He lived on a farm called Popes Creek.

3. His family moved to Mount Vernon, Virginia, when he was three.

4. Later, George Washington lived near the town of Fredericksburg.

5. George Washington married Martha Custis in 1759.

6. He led the American army during a war.

7. George Washington was elected the first President of the United States.

8. President's Day is a holiday that honors him and other Presidents.

0-7424-1857-X *Grammar Basics Plus*

Name ______________________________ Date ______________________

Proper Nouns

A **proper noun** names a special person, place, or thing. All proper nouns begin with capital letters. Some proper nouns are made with more than one word.

Directions: Read the letter. Write proper nouns to complete it.

(your name) ______________________________
(your address) ______________________________
(your city, state) ______________________________

George Washington Birthplace National Monument
1732 Popes Creek Road
Washington's Birthplace, Virginia 22443

Dear Park Ranger Bohls,

I am writing a report on our first president, George Washington. I have read all of the books in the library at our school, (your school name) ______________________________. I have even looked in the bookstore (a bookstore name) ______________________________. But I have not found much information on the life of George Washington when he was a boy. Could you please send me a brochure about his life at Popes Creek? I know he was born there.

Sincerely,
(your name) ______________________________

Name ______________________________ Date ______________

Abbreviations of Names and Places

An **abbreviation** is a short way to write a proper noun. All abbreviations begin with a capital letter. They end in a period. Some abbreviations of titles are **Mr**., **Mrs**., and **Dr**. Some abbreviations of places are **Rd**. (Road), **Dr**. (Drive), **Ave**. (Avenue), and **St**. (Street).

Example: Doctor Louis is a sports doctor.
Dr. Louis is a sports doctor.

Directions: Read the sentences. Underline the word that can be written as an abbreviation in each sentence. Then write the abbreviation on the line.

1. Dr. Louis has an office on Burnet Road. ______________

2. Mister Ken Parker will go see the doctor. ______________

3. Ken Parker leaves his house on West Street. ______________

4. He turns onto Westlake Drive. ______________

5. He passes the hospital on Shoal Creek Avenue. ______________

6. Ken sees Doctor Alma Richards walking out the door. ______________

Name ______________________ Date ______________

Abbreviations of Names and Places

An **abbreviation** is a short way to write a proper noun. All abbreviations begin with a capital letter. They end in a period. Some abbreviations of titles are **Mr**., **Mrs**., and **Dr**. Some abbreviations of places are **Rd**. (Road), **Dr**. (Drive), **Ave**. (Avenue), and **St**. (Street).

Directions: Read the directions. Write the correct abbreviation of the word in parentheses ( ) on the line.

To: **(1)** (Mister) __________ Todd Jenkins

From: Miss Ella Hao

Directions to **(2)** (Doctor) __________ Andrea Mills's office:

1. Drive north for 5 miles on Ranch **(3)** (Road) __________
2. Turn left onto Canyon **(4)** (Drive) __________ and go 3 miles.
3. Turn right onto Slope **(5)** (Street) __________
4. Take the second right at Cattle **(6)** (Avenue) __________
5. **(7)** (Doctor) __________ Mills's office is in Building 2.

Let me know what **(8)** (Doctor) __________ Mills says. I hope all goes well.

Sincerely,

Ella

Name ______________________ Date ______________

Abbreviations of Days and Months

An **abbreviation** is a short way to write a proper noun. All abbreviations begin with a capital letter. They end with a period. The names of the days of the week can be abbreviated. The names of the months of the year can be abbreviated, too.

Sunday	Sun.	January	Jan.	July	Jul.
Monday	Mon.	February	Feb.	August	Aug.
Tuesday	Tues.	March	Mar.	September	Sept.
Wednesday	Wed.	April	Apr.	October	Oct.
Thursday	Thurs.	May	May	November	Nov.
Friday	Fri.	June	Jun.	December	Dec.
Saturday	Sat.				

Example: Independence Day is Tuesday, July 4.
Independence Day is Tues., Jul. 4.

Directions: Read the sentences. Underline the word or words that can be written as an abbreviation in each sentence. Then write the abbreviations.

1. President's Day is always the third Monday in February. ______________

____

2. Mother's Day is the second Sunday in May. ______________

____

3. Halloween always falls on October 31. ______________

4. This year, Halloween will be on Friday. ______________

0-7424-1857-X *Grammar Basics Plus*

Name ______________________________ Date ______________

Abbreviations of Days and Months

An **abbreviation** is a short way to write a proper noun. All abbreviations begin with a capital letter. They end with a period. The names of the days of the week and the months of the year can be abbreviated.

Directions: Read the letter. Write the correct abbreviation of the word in parentheses ( ) on the line.

(1) (August) ____________ 27, 2003

Dear Grandma,

It is (2) (Wednesday) ____________ evening now. There are only three more days until the big softball championship on (3) (Saturday) ____________ The season started back in (4) (April) ____________, so I am ready for it to be over. We practice each (5) (Monday) ____________ and (6) (Thursday) ____________ We have games each weekend. I am looking forward to spending some free time with my friends.

Dad says that you might drive down this weekend to watch the game. I hope you will be able to come. If not, I know I will see you in (7) (October) ____________ for my birthday. I will also visit you in (8) (December) ____________ for Hanukkah.

Love,

Sara

Name ______________________________ Date ______________

Names of Holidays and Historical Events

The names of **holidays** are proper nouns. The names of **events** and **important papers** in history are proper nouns, too. They all begin with a capital letter.

Examples:

Event:	America was divided during the Civil War.
Important paper:	The Kansas-Nebraska Act let people in those states decide to be free or to have slaves.
Holiday:	Memorial Day is an important holiday to remember those who fought.

Directions: Read the sentences. Underline the proper noun in each sentence. Tell if the noun is a holiday, an event, or an important paper.

1. The Battle of Bull Run was the first big battle between the states. ______________________

2. President Lincoln signed the Emancipation Proclamation to free slaves. ______________________

3. The Battle of Shiloh was a turning point in the war. ______________________

4. Lincoln wrote a famous speech called the Gettysburg Address. ______________________

5. The U.S. Constitution was changed to end slavery. ______________________

6. Some states in the South celebrate Confederate Day. ______________________

Name ______________________________ Date ____________________

Names of Holidays and Historical Events

The names of **holidays** are proper nouns. The names of **events** and **important papers** in history are proper nouns, too. They all begin with a capital letter.

Directions: Read the story. Then rewrite each underlined name correctly on the lines below.

The Museum Trip

Paula loved going to the museum. Last Saturday, she visited the floor that showed things from the **(1)** american revolution. She had read the **(2)** declaration of independence. This weekend Paula wanted to visit the floor that showed the **(3)** civil war. There was a special exhibit about the **(4)** battle of fredericksburg. Also, she heard that a copy of Abraham Lincoln's **(5)** gettysburg address was there.

When Paula got to the museum, the door would not open. A sign said, "Closed for **(6)** labor day."

"Oh, no!" exclaimed Paula. "I forgot that today was a holiday! I will have to wait until next weekend to visit."

(1) ____________________

(2) ____________________

(3) ____________________

(4) ____________________

(5) ____________________

(6) ____________________

Name ______________________ Date ______________

Titles

The **titles** of books, magazines, movies, and newspapers are underlined or put in *italics*. The titles of book chapters, stories, and articles are put in quotation marks.

Examples: Magazine title: National Geographic is an interesting magazine.

Article: The article "A Dinosaur Named Sue" told about an important dinosaur fossil.

Directions: Read the sentences. Underline the titles of books. Write quotation marks around minor titles.

1. The Chicago Tribune also wrote an article about the dinosaur called Sue.

2. This article was called Run Around Sue.

3. The author, Steve Fiffer, wrote a book called Tyrannosaurus Sue.

4. This book was a favorite on the New York Times book list for several weeks.

5. Children also learned about Sue in the book The Field Mouse and the Dinosaur Named Sue.

6. The cartoon movie The Land Before Time was about dinosaurs.

7. Another movie called Dinosaur appeared in theaters more recently.

Name ________________________________ Date ____________________

Titles

The **titles** of books, magazines, movies, and newspapers are underlined or put in *italics*. The titles of book chapters, stories, and articles are put in quotation marks.

Directions: Read the story. Look at the words in parentheses ( ). Then rewrite the words correctly on the lines.

Mrs. Kent walked into the room and stopped. "Why is this mess all over the floor?" she asked.

Adam looked a little guilty. "I am doing a current event report for school. I was looking in the **(1)** (West End Post) for an interesting article. I found one titled **(2)** (Theater Time). It is a review of the new movie **(3)** (Dinosaur Days)."

"How is this a current event?" Mrs. Kent asked.

"The movie was made from my teacher's favorite children's book, **(4)** (Lives of Dinosaurs)," said Adam. "I thought my teacher would like to know what people are currently saying about the movie."

"I don't think that is what Mr. Arnold meant by current events," said Mrs. Kent. "But I think you need to do a current event yourself. Please clean up this mess!"

(1) ____

(2) ____

(3) ____

(4) ____

Name ______________________________ Date ______________

Difficult Words

Some words are difficult to spell. They do not follow the spelling rules we know. Some people call these words "elephant words." We must remember how to spell the words.

Example: Incorrect: Thair are nine planets in the solar system.
Correct: There are nine planets in the solar system.

Directions: Read the sentences. Circle the word that correctly completes each sentence.

1. Mercury is the planet that is (close, cloze) to the sun.
2. Venus is one planet that is (visable, visible) in the night sky.
3. Earth is the only planet where life can (eksist, exist).
4. Mars is the (forfth, fourth) planet from the sun.
5. Jupiter has (fierce, fearce) storms that blow on it.
6. Saturn is a planet that has (several, sevrul) rings and moons.
7. Uranus and Neptune were (discovered, discuverd) using a telescope.
8. Pluto is the planet that is the greatest (distunce, distance) from the sun.

0-7424-1857-X *Grammar Basics Plus*

Name ______________________ Date ______________

Difficult Words

Some words are difficult to spell. They do not follow the spelling rules we know. Some people call these words "elephant words." We must remember how to spell the words.

Directions: Read the story. Circle the word that correctly completes the sentences.

Erh-Lang and the Seven Sons

Long ago in China, seven suns were the rulers of the sky. Their rays beat down on the villagers and made them hot. The crops in the **(1)** (feelds, fields) began to die.

Finally, the **(2)** (people, peeple) asked the wise woman how to keep the suns from causing so much damage.

The woman **(3)** (thawt, thought) for a moment. "Go ask Erh-Lang," she **(4)** (ansered, answered). "He is very strong."

Ehr-Lang agreed to help. **(5)** (Early, Ehrly) the next day, Ehr-Lang waited for the suns to rise. When the first sun began to shine, he grabbed it and placed it inside a mountain. He did the same with the next five suns. Slowly, the heat and light began to **(6)** (disapeer, disappear). The seventh sun saw what happened. He stayed **(7)** (safely, sayfly) hidden underground.

The wise woman had another idea. She called to the birds, "Sing sweetly to the sun so he will come out."

The sun **(8)** (heard, hurd) the birds and came out from its hiding place. Everyone began to cheer. To this day, the birds sing every morning to ask the sun to come out.

Name ______________________ Date ______________

Unit 3 Assessment

Directions: Read the sentences. Write each sentence correctly. Use correct capitalization and punctuation.

1. do you know who invented the telephone

____

2. dr alexander graham bell invented the telephone

____

3. he made the first call to mr tom watson on march 10, 1876

____

4. bell said mr watson, come here. I want you

____

Directions: Read the sentences. Circle the word that correctly completes each sentence.

5. Immediately, telephones became a popular (masheen, machine).

6. Telephone wires crossed the (country, cuntree).

7. (Millions, Milyuns) of people put phones in their homes.

8. Today, people can (carry, carrie) phones with them wherever they go.

Name ______________________________ Date ______________

Unit 3 Assessment

Directions: Read the sentences. Rewrite each sentence correctly. Look for spelling, capitalization, and punctuation mistakes. (Hint: There are two mistakes in each sentence.)

1. Marco did not go to school on monday because it was president's day.

____

2. He was looking through the Oak Hill Times to see when the movie Baseball Fever started.

____

3. An article called Important Machines caught his interest.

____

4. In the article, Dr Laura Baker listed the most important inventions of the century

____

5. Most people thawht the computer was the most important invention

____

6. "I think video games should be on the list said Marco.

____

Answer Key

What Is a Noun? ....page 6
1. thing
2. place
3. thing
4. person
5. place
6. thing

What Is a Noun? ....page 7
Answer order may vary.
Person
man
cowboys
people

Place
woods
state
desert

Thing
rattlesnake
cow
lasso

Common Nouns............page 8
1. place
2. place
3. thing
4. person
5. place
6. thing

Common Nouns............page 9
1. pie
2. judge
3. paper
4. fair
5. friends
6. prize
7. winner
8. bakery

Proper Nouns ....page 10
1. Amelia, Kansas
2. California
3. Neta Snook
4. Amelia, Atlantic Ocean
5. Vega
6. Ameila
7. United States
8. Amelia, New Guinea

Proper Nouns ....page 11
Answers will vary.

Singular and Plural Nouns ....page 12
1. wings; plural
2. head; singular
3. beak; singular
4. bugs; plural
5. nest; singular
6. eggs; plural

Singular and Plural Nouns ....page 13
Answer order may vary.
Singular Nouns
river
nest

Plural Nouns
feathers
eggs

Plural Nouns ....page 14
1. benches
2. stories
3. boxes
4. families
5. babies
6. classes
7. lunches
8. bags

Plural Nouns ....page 15
1. dishes
2. glasses
3. boxes
4. branches
5. bushes
6. foxes
7. friends

Possessive Nouns.........page 16
1. slide's
2. boys'
3. women's
4. baby's
5. team's
6. girls'
7. boy's
8. children's

Possessive Nouns.........page 17
1. playground's
2. girls'
3. people's
4. puppies'
5. Gina's
6. friends'
7. Gina's
8. girls'

What Is a Verb?............page 18
1. crawl
2. swim
3. eats
4. looks
5. sheds
6. grows
7. hide
8. eat

What Is a Verb?............page 19
1. serves
2. gives
3. send
4. fights
5. battle
6. crawls
7. bite
8. crush

Verbs ....page 20
1. eats
2. walk
3. like
4. swims
5. holds
6. helps
7. flap
8. cools

Answer Key

Verbs ....page 21
1. asks
2. lifts
3. walk
4. crawls
5. return
6. play

Linking Verbs................page 22
1. was
2. were
3. was
4. was
5. were
6. are
7. is
8. is

Linking Verbs................page 23
1. is
2. was
3. was
4. was
5. were
6. is
7. am

Helping Verbs ....page 24
1. had lived; had
2. were working; were
3. did dream; did
4. was worried; was
5. was going; was
6. had planned; had
7. have found; have
8. will remember; will

Helping Verbs ....page 25
1. was
2. had
3. were
4. am
5. was
6. will
7. will
8. is
9. am

The Verb *Be* (*Am*, *Is*, and *Are*) ....page 26
1. are
2. are
3. are
4. is
5. is
6. are
7. are
8. is

The Verb *Be* (*Am*, *Is*, and *Are*) ....page 27
1. are
2. are
3. is
4. is
5. am
6. are

The Verb *Be* (*Was* and *Were*) ....page 28
1. was
2. was
3. were
4. was
5. were
6. was
7. were
8. were

The Verb *Be* (*Was* and *Were*) ....page 29
1. was
2. were
3. was
4. was
5. were
6. were

Present Tense Verbs ....page 30
1. mixes
2. wishes
3. splash
4. paint
5. fuss
6. dries
7. touches
8. sell

Present Tense Verbs ....page 31
1. teaches
2. watch
3. try
4. fusses
5. matches
6. wants

Past Tense Verbs ....page 32
1. honored
2. gathered
3. raced
4. added
5. boxed
6. pulled
7. cheered
8. lasted

Past Tense Verbs ....page 33
1. talked
2. laughed
3. decided
4. walked
5. curled
6. crossed

Future Tense Verbs ......page 34
1. will toss
2. will dump
3. will go
4. will take
5. will recycle
6. will reuse
7. will find
8. will reduce

Future Tense Verbs ......page 35
1. will find
2. will do
3. will reuse
4. will ride
5. will recycle
6. will wash

Answer Key

Verb Agreement..........page 36
1. drop; plural
2. travel; plural
3. moves; singular
4. catch; plural
5. blows; singular
6. carry; plural
7. falls; singular
8. grows; singular

Verb Agreement..........page 37
1. runs
2. stick
3. look
4. climb
5. follows
6. grow

Irregular Verbs ....page 38
1. left
2. knew
3. took
4. wrote
5. begin
6. come
7. bring
8. make

Irregular Verbs ....page 39
1. began
2. thought
3. met
4. went
5. go
6. run

What Is a Prounoun?...page 40
1. They
2. She
3. He
4. They
5. It
6. They
7. they
8. it

What Is a Prounoun?...page 41
1. We
2. It
3. He
4. it
5. They
6. They
7. you
8. it

Subject and Object Pronouns..........page 42
1. She
2. them
3. they
4. her
5. them
6. him

Subject and Object Pronouns..........page 43
1. I
2. it
3. her
4. She
5. they
6. he
7. She
8. them

Possessive Pronouns....page 44
1. his
2. her
3. its
4. Their
5. their
6. its
7. your
8. my

Possessive Pronouns....page 45
1. his
2. its
3. his
4. Its
5. his
6. my
7. her
8. their

Demonstrative Pronouns.......................page 46
1. That
2. Those
3. These
4. this
5. this
6. that
7. those
8. these

Demonstrative Pronouns.......................page 47
1. This
2. Those
3. That
4. Those
5. these

Interrogative Pronouns.......................page 48
1. which
2. Whose
3. Who
4. What
5. Whom
6. Who
7. whom
8. What

Interrogative Pronouns.......................page 49
Most likely answers are given.
1. Whose
2. Which
3. Who
4. what
5. Whom

Answer Key

Antecedents................page 50
1. underline: They; circle: Americans
2. underline: It; circle: resin
3. underline: He; circle: William Wrigley
4. underline: They; circle: Americans
5. underline: It; circle: gum
6. underline: They; circle: salesmen

Antecedents................page 51
1. Gina
2. bubble
3. Beth
4. Tyler
5. bubble
6. pink

What Is an Adjective?....................page 52
1. five
2. 35
3. female
4. old
5. 40
6. lazy
7. small
8. Brown

What Is an Adjective?....................page 53
1. greatest
2. green
3. five
4. long
5. one
6. strong

Adjectives That Compare.....................page 54
1. big
2. bigger
3. biggest
4. ferocious
5. more ferocious
6. most ferocious
7. funny
8. funniest

Adjectives That Compare.....................page 55
1. most intelligent
2. larger
3. faster
4. better
5. bigger
6. biggest
7. loudest
8. funniest

Adverbs........................page 56
1. swiftly
2. Suddenly
3. loudly
4. Then
5. safely
6. heavily
7. later
8. brightly

Adverbs........................page 57
1. Lately
2. swiftly
3. today
4. suddenly
5. dangerously
6. Soon

Use *Good* and *Well*.....page 58
1. good
2. good
3. well
4. good
5. well
6. well
7. good
8. good, good

Use *Good* and *Well*.....page 59
1. well
2. good
3. good
4. well
5. good
6. well
7. good
8. good

Prepositions ....page 60
1. in
2. between
3. to
4. on
5. for
6. about
7. to
8. From

Prepositions ....page 61
Answers may vary. Possible answers are given.
1. to
2. over
3. as
4. of
5. around
6. of
7. from
8. for

Conjunctions...............page 62
1. and
2. or
3. but
4. but
5. or
6. but
7. and
8. or

Conjunctions...............page 63
1. and
2. or
3. but
4. and
5. but
6. but
7. and
8. or

Answer Key

Simple and Complex Sentences .... page 64

Answers may vary. Possible answers are given.

1. Apples can be red or green.
2. Oranges are sweet and juicy.
3. People eat the skin of apples, but not the skin of oranges.
4. Apples and oranges are fruits.

Simple and Complex Sentences .... page 65

1. and
2. or
3. but
4. but
5. and
6. but
7. and
8. but

Interjections .... page 66

1. Great
2. Ouch
3. Oops
4. Oh
5. Aha
6. Whew
7. Yay
8. Hurray

Interjections .... page 67

Answer order may vary. Possible answers are given.

1. Wow
2. Gee
3. Yikes
4. Oh
5. Aha
6. Great

Unit 1 Assessment .... page 68

1. adjective
2. pronoun
3. adverb
4. verb
5. conjunction
6. noun
7. preposition
8. interjection

Unit 1 Assessment........ page 69

1. He
2. tornado
3. biggest
4. and
5. sat
6. Wow
7. off
8. more
9. his
10. poured
11. Today
12. scared

Subject and Verb Agreement .... page 70

1. circle: ocean; underline: falls; singular
2. circle: Treasures; underline: lay; plural
3. circle: people; underline: walk; plural
4. circle: people; underline: hunt; plural
5. circle: child; underline: picks; singular
6. circle: people; underline: look; plural
7. circle: person; underline: finds; singular
8. circle: visitors; underline: stay; plural

Subject and Verb Agreement .... page 71

1. help
2. use
3. like
4. grab
5. pushes
6. moves
7. were
8. appears

Verb Tense .... page 72

1. circle: stacked; past
2. circle: warmed; past
3. circle: designs; present
4. circle: move; present
5. circle: will be; future
6. circle: will build; future

Verb Tense .... page 73

1. settled
2. planted
3. want
4. join
5. will eat
6. will play

Irregular Verbs .... page 74

1. began; past
2. went; past
3. won; past
4. saw; past
5. sell; present
6. throws; present
7. swings; present
8. catch; present

Irregular Verbs .... page 75

1. caught
2. got
3. ran
4. comes
5. see
6. swings
7. flies
8. find

Present

comes
see
swings
flies
find

Past

caught
got
ran

Pronouns and Antecedents .... page 76

1. They wanted to be free from British rule.
2. He led the American soldiers.
3. They fought the British.
4. She sewed the first American flag.
5. We have freedom because of those brave Americans.

Answer Key

Pronouns and Antecedents................page 77
1. Americans
2. Betsy Ross
3. George Washington
4. George and Betsy
5. flag
6. flag
7. You and I

Prefixes.........................page 78
1. uncertain—not certain
2. misspelled—not spelled correctly
3. retype—type again
4. undo—opposite of do
5. preview—view before

Prefixes.........................page 79
1. unhappy
2. unusual
3. rewrite
4. unable
5. dislike
6. preview
7. rejoin
8. misuse

Suffixes ....page 80
1. loudly—in a loud way
2. marchers—ones who march
3. happily—in a happy way
4. careful—full of care
5. careless—without care

Suffixes ....page 81
1. countless
2. careless
3. leader
4. loudly
5. colorful
6. happily
7. speechless

Synonyms ....page 82
1. argued
2. leader
3. desired
4. peacefully
5. talked
6. join
7. contented
8. discovered

Synonyms ....page 83
1. sons
2. attempted
3. bundle
4. break
5. strength
6. divided

Antonyms.....................page 84
1. great
2. together
3. leader
4. up
5. loudly
6. sick
7. quickly
8. dangerous

Antonyms.....................page 85
1. funny
2. quickly
3. up
4. top
5. angrily
6. come

Compound Words ......page 86
1. sail + boat
2. swim + suit
3. camp + fire
4. base + ball
5. play + ground

Compound Words ......page 87
1. treehouse
2. notebook
3. bluebird
4. butterfly
5. rainbow
6. inchworm

Homophones...............page 88
1. see
2. tail
3. night
4. to
5. berries
6. roots
7. chews
8. hear

Homophones...............page 89
1. One
2. hours
3. find
4. main
5. hear
6. know
7. to
8. way
9. hear
10. where

Homographs...............page 90
Letter order is shown.
1. b, a
2. a, b
3. b, a
4. b, a

Homographs...............page 91
1. d
2. c
3. f
4. a
5. b
6. e

Answer Key

Troublesome Words ....page 92

1. too
2. Their
3. They're
4. two
5. to
6. there
7. their, to
8. too

Troublesome Words ....page 93

1. There
2. two
3. there
4. too
5. there
6. to
7. two
8. their
9. their
10. their
11. They're
12. to

Contractions.................page 94

1. Most plants won't grow during the winter.
2. They don't get enough heat to help them grow.
3. They usually can't get enough water either.
4. To grow plants in the winter, you'll need a greenhouse.
5. It's a see-through building where plants stay warm all year long.

Contractions.................page 95

1. couldn't
2. I'm
3. it's
4. wouldn't
5. weren't
6. They'll
7. she'd

Double Negatives ....page 96

1. circle: don't, nobody; Famous people, such as movie stars, don't want anybody to recognize them.
2. circle: can't, hardly; They can't go outside without adoring fans bothering them.
3. circle: nothing, nobody; Once a star is seen, there's nothing anybody can do.
4. circle: won't, no; The star won't go to that place any more.
5. circle: never, nobody; They will never again tell anybody where they are going.

Double Negatives ....page 97

Answers may vary.

Tamara could hardly believe her luck.

Tamara hadn't been allowed to tell anybody, though.

So I can't take anybody else!

So Tamara hadn't said anything.

Jewels didn't give autographs to anyone.

No one would believe me if I did show the autograph anyway.

Unit 2 Assessment ....page 98

1. lived
2. kept
3. visit
4. will learn
5. can't hardly; possible answer: Visitors can't believe how people lived long ago.
6. not, no; possible answer: The people did not have running water.
7. They
8. It

Unit 2 Assessment ....page 99

1. wet
2. tiny
3. fantastic
4. many
5. to
6. their
7. disliked
8. happily

Sentence Endings......page 100

Answers may vary.

1. . (declarative)
2. ? (interrogative)
3. . (declarative)
4. ! (exclamation)
5. . (command)
6. ! (exclamation)

Sentence Endings......page 101

Answers may vary.

1. ?
2. .
3. .
4. !
5. !
6. ?
7. ?
8. .

Commas.....................page 102

Commas are underlined.

1. The flies lay their eggs on the ground, on the water, or on other animals.
2. Then, the eggs hatch into the larva stage.
3. The larva live in rotting plants, food, or garbage.
4. Most larva eat, grow, and build a cocoon.
5. Next, the larva becomes a pupa, and changes to look like an adult fly.
6. Finally, the adult fly breaks out of the cocoon.

Answer Key

Commas....................page 103

Corrections are underlined.

Long ago, there was a beautiful river that flowed through the land. The water was clear, cool, and clean. Many of the land animals came to drink from it.

One day, a moose came to drink from the water. The moose was a huge animal and drank large amounts of the water. The water quickly disappeared because the moose came to drink each day.

The animals met to discuss the problem. "What shall we do they asked?" Moose was so big that all the animals were afraid to talk to him.

Then, the fly decided to drive moose away. "I am small," said Fly. "Moose will not see me!" So, Fly went to the river the next morning and waited for Moose. When Moose lowered his head to drink, Fly bit him on the leg. Moose stamped his foot hard and left a deep hole that filled with water.

Next, Fly bit moose on his hind foot. Moose stamped again, making another hole. Fly continued to bite Moose all over. Moose stamped, shook, and twisted to get rid of Fly, but nothing worked. Finally, Moose ran away from the river and did not return.

"I may be small," said Fly. "But I am very smart!"

Quotation Marks........page 104

Check that students circle each quotation mark and underline each comma, period, question mark, and exclamation point.

Quotation Marks........page 105

1. !
2. ?
3. ,
4. "
5. ,
6. "
7. !
8. "

Proper Nouns ....page 106

1. George Washington, February
2. Popes Creek
3. Mount Vernon, Virginia
4. George Washington, Fredericksburg
5. George Washington, Martha Custis
6. American
7. George Washington, President, United States
8. President's Day, Presidents

Proper Nouns ....page 107

Answers will vary. Check to see that students use a capital letter to write proper nouns.

Abbreviations of Names and Places.................page 108

1. Road; Rd.
2. Mister; Mr.
3. Street; St.
4. Drive; Dr.
5. Avenue; Ave.
6. Doctor; Dr.

Abbreviations of Names and Places.................page 109

1. Mr.
2. Dr.
3. Rd.
4. Dr.
5. St.
6. Ave.
7. Dr.
8. Dr.

Abbreviations of Days and Months ....page 110

1. Mon.; Feb.
2. Sun.
3. Oct.
4. Fri.

Abbreviations of Days and Months ....page 111

1. Aug.
2. Wed.
3. Sat.
4. Apr.
5. Mon.
6. Thurs.
7. Oct.
8. Dec.

Names of Holidays and Historical Events ....page 112

1. Battle of Bull Run; event
2. Emancipation Proclamation; paper
3. Battle of Shiloh; event
4. Gettysburg Address; paper
5. United States Constitution; paper
6. Confederate Day; holiday

Names of Holidays and Historical Events ....page 113

1. American Revolution
2. Declaration of Independence
3. Civil War
4. Battle of Fredericksburg
5. Gettysburg Address
6. Labor Day

Titles ....page 114

1. underline: Chicago Tribune
2. quotation marks: "Run Around Sue."
3. underline: Tyrannosaurus Sue
4. underline: The New York Times
5. underline: The Field Mouse and the Dinosaur Named Sue
6. underline: The Land Before Time
7. underline: Dinosaur

Answer Key

Titles ....page 115

1. *West End Post (underlined)*
2. "Theater Time"
3. *Dinosaur Days (underlined)*
4. *Lives of Dinosaurs (underlined)*

Difficult Words ....page 116

1. close
2. visible
3. exist
4. fourth
5. fierce
6. several
7. discovered
8. distance

Difficult Words ....page 117

1. fields
2. people
3. thought
4. answered
5. early
6. disappear
7. safely
8. heard

Unit 3 Assessment ......page 118

1. Do you know who invented the telephone?
2. Dr. Alexander Graham Bell invented the telephone.
3. He made the first call to Mr. Tom Watson on March 10, 1876.
4. Bell said, "Mr. Watson, come here. I want you."
5. machine
6. country
7. Millions
8. carry

Unit 3 Assessment ......page 119

Corrections are underlined.

1. Marco did not go to school on Monday because it was President's Day.
2. He was looking through the Oak Hill Times to see when the movie Baseball Fever started.
3. An article called "Important Machines" caught his interest.
4. In the article, Dr. Laura Baker listed the most important inventions of the century.
5. Most people thought the computer was the most important invention.
6. "I think video games should be on the list," said Marco.